Image credits:

CW00676701

Cover image by Ann Massey O'Regan

Interior images courtesy of Dominic McElroy and Ann Massey O'Regan

'Fear Darrig" 'The Banshee' Public Domain

DARK EMERALD TALES

By

Ann Massey O'Regan

Fear Darrig

Published by

Greenock, Scotland

ISBN - 978-0-9957784-2-9

CONTENTS

FOREWORD

The great blues guitarist B.B King once said, *"I don't think anybody steals anything, all of us borrow."* Never a truer word has been spoken when it comes to folklore and tales of hauntings. Tales have been 'borrowed' and written about by so many over centuries in Ireland, often with no clue as to the original source.

In an ancient nation with such diverse history, accounts have become stories that have not just been handed down through generations but meandered over regions and through years of religious and national upheaval and bloodshed.

If anyone tells you they have the definitive 'facts' regarding a haunting tale or a folklore story, they are lying. Every story changes depending on who tells it and for me, that is the wonder of Irish folklore and hauntings. You never hear the same tale twice, it is often 'borrowed' from castle to castle and town to town, but the basis in Irish history remains the same.

Every dark account of a haunting, every tale of a legend or a creature from the faery realm starts with a simple seed of truth. That seed is nurtured and watered, the care of an account passed on from generation to generation, until it blossoms into a magical, mystical and often downright terrifying folklore masterpiece.

We are a nation who 'believe.' Whether it is faith in a deity, from Pagan to Christian, in the festivals of protection and prosperity, a ghostly figure in a castle window or the cry of the Banshee to warn of a loved one's passing, we believe. The most hardened cynic or skeptic may try and convince you it's all nonsense, but whether they would destroy a fairy fort and still sleep at night is another matter! Because deep down that is how we were raised – these tales are in our blood, our culture and our national heritage.

For me as I sat as a child and listening to my mum tell me stories of ghosts and ethereal beings, I believed and to this day I still do. My own experiences have fuelled that belief and interest and I will never stop seeking these extraordinary accounts and tales. The beauty of actual historic fact being so wonderfully mixed with superstition, religious belief and personal experiences, creates an ever-evolving legacy of creativity and passion, stamped with a seal of approval that simply says 'Ireland, the magical Emerald Isle.'

Welcome to my Dark Emerald Tales.

Ann Massey O'Regan

MAGIC, MYTHS & MONSTERS – WELCOME TO THE DARK EMERALD ISLE

For generations, children of Ireland have been reared on mythology and folklore. Of course, to us they are far more than the tales of ancient legends, they are where we come from and define who we are now. From Cú Chulainn and Fionn mac Cumhaill, to the triple goddess, The Morrigan, giants, demi gods and creatures from the ethereal realm have always been a part of our lives.

Most of Ireland's regional and national festivals evolved from the gods and goddesses of ancient times. None more so than the Tuatha Dé Danann, deities deemed as the forefathers of Irish culture and civilization. The Formorians, a wild and altogether darker and more sinister supernatural race, still had their part to play.

Fear is at the source of most of folklore tales and practices, particularly in relation to death and the protection of the soul as well as safeguarding against the ethereal creatures of darkness. The festival of Samhain is a prime example, taking place at the end of October intertwining the light and dark, shielding against bad spirits and misfortune, but also welcoming back the dead with open arms.

The fear for celebrants was that malevolent spirits and evil entities could also cross with their loved ones, as could the Devil himself. As well as the dead, homeowners had to contend with the fairies travelling abroad to create mischief. Gifts in the form of food or milk would be left on doorsteps to guarantee a fairy blessing and anyone foolish enough to not do so would be subject to pranks by the cheeky wee folk at best and victim to a fairy curse at worst.

Without a doubt, the most terrifying of these supernatural beings are the harbingers of death. *Crom Dubh* was the sacrificial god associated with death and slaughter and his incarnation was The Dullahan, a part of the Unseelie Court of the fairy realm. The Unseelie fairies are those deemed the most evil and malicious of all the otherworld entities. Also known as *Gan Ceann*, meaning without a head, The Dullahan hunts the souls of the dying in the night.

Banshees have forever been known as portents of death and the goddess Clíodhna was the very first of these wailing spirits seeking death for revenge and torment as well as calling on those due to die. Individual families often having their own personal Banshee heralding a death to this very day.

From these gods and goddesses an entire culture and belief system has grown, with Ireland being home to a myriad of ethereal creatures and spirits, from both the 'good' Seelie Court and 'sinister' Unseelie Court.

Once again, fear is the driving force behind the behaviour and response to these creatures and their accompanying threat, with fortification rites being fundamental. Druidic runes for example focus on strength, energy, health and protection. The markings on runes tend to come from Ogham, an ancient language of Ireland uncovered by archaeological finds over the centuries by way of Ogham Stones. These Stones have been found all over Ireland, usually associated with burial stones of ancient kings and warriors, however they are not of the past – Druidic practices are not just ongoing in modern Ireland but growing in popularity.

In previous centuries, much of the population of Ireland couldn't read or write and hexes, protection spells and rituals involved symbolism to get the point across. A *Piseóg* is a curse, placed on feuding neighbours, competing farmers and so on. Often recognized by a circle of eggs found in the hay or a talisman placed on a wall, they are set to bring misfortune on the home.

What of the cute and friendly leprechaun? Don't kid yourself! There are several types of leprechaun and not all of them guard a crock of gold! Around for over 1000 years, the leprechaun is descended from the Tuatha Dé Danann and are a part of the *Sidhe* or Fairy family. The name Leprechaun has two sources, both from old Irish. The first is *Leath Bhrogan*, meaning shoemaker and the second is *Luacharmán* meaning small body.

Leprechauns like to keep themselves to themselves and really don't like mortals – or each other. Very much loners they are happiest in their own intoxicated company, however there is one you should be afraid of and that is the *Fear Dearg*, which translates as 'Red Man'. Recognized by his blemished yellowy skin, *Fear Dearg* is dressed head to foot in red and his greatest delight is your fear and dread. He has the ability to make your nightmare a reality.

This is all just the tip of the iceberg. We have Fairy Shock Troops riding the wind, devastating farmlands and cattle just for kicks, spirits of the eternally damned wandering the earthly realm looking for Irish souls to steal, serpents, mermaids and hellhounds. We have the *Púca*, a shapeshifting creature who terrorizes the night and ghosts, demons and the Devil himself.

If you thought Saint Patrick had driven all the paganism and darkness from Ireland, you would be wrong. Far from Christianity banishing these beliefs and rituals, the early monks documented these mythological events into such manuscripts as the *Book of Leinster* and the *Annals of the Four Provinces*. Instead of turning the Irish away from their gods and goddesses, the clergy fashioned their stories into those of Saints such as Saint Brigid. Christian and Pagan stories are intertwined in much the same way Irish history and mythology can never be separated, and why we are great storytellers - it's in our blood, heritage and very essence of being.

Ireland is a land rich in mythology and folklore, mixed with dark history and truth, bound neatly in fear, magic and excitement. Welcome to the Emerald Isle!

GODS, LEGENDS AND FEASTS

Gods, Myths and Mortals of the Emerald Isle

When it comes to Irish history, there is a point where 'fact' takes a backseat and tales of legendary heroes and villains take centre stage. What did you expect? We are a nation of storytellers!

While the races of the Tuatha Dé Danann and the Formorians are known worldwide, many forget that the Fir Bolg, or 'Men of the Bog' were long settled on the desolate Irish landscape. Do not let the translation of the name fool you – it simply means they were able to turn rocky barren fields into fertile, arable lands. These literal and figurative groundbreaking men also established the sacred Hill of Tara and were the first of the High Kings of Ireland.

It is little wonder therefore, that a race of demi-gods, descendants of the goddess Dana, mother of the land, would take an interest in conquering a domain of such opportunity. So it was that several decades after the Fir Bolg were settled, the Tuatha Dé Danann rode on the wind and came down from the sky and set foot in the Emerald Isle.

The number four is paramount throughout any documented accounts of the Tuatha Dé Danann. They created four cities, Falias, Gorias, Finias and Marias. They had four wise men to teach their youth both skills and knowledge, for without both they could not know wisdom. Each city had its own treasure, the keystones of the Tuatha Dé Danann – the Stone of Virtue, which called to the King of Ireland; the Sword from which, no man could escape once drawn; the Spear of Victory; and the Magic Cauldron, which left no appetite unsated.

Nuada was the King of the Tuatha Dé Danann. Around him, he had great men such as Ogma, teacher of the written word; Dian Cecht, an incredible physician; Goibniu the Smith; and Credenus the ultimate Craftsman. Also on the great warrior's team were his own gods: Neit, the god of Battle and the Morrigan, triple goddess of war, fertility and sovereignty.

It is said that the mighty Tuatha Dé Danann arrived in the Province of Connaught on the first day of the feast of Beltaine. The Ancient Druids told the King of the Fir Bolg, Eochaid, that his dreams foretold of a powerful enemy approaching. He sent his Champion,

Sreng to meet with the emissary of the Tuatha Dé Danann known as Bres. An interesting side note is that Bres was of mixed race - Tuatha Dé Danann and Formorian, a fact that will become of much relevance soon.

Sreng informed Bres that the weapon he carried was called 'Craisech' and it would cut through flesh and bone, no shield was capable fending it off, and the wounds it inflicted would never heal. An offer was made to the Fir Bolg that they could settle in one part of Ireland and leave the rest to the mighty Tuatha Dé Danann, an offer that was refused. And so began the First Battle of Magh Tuireadh.

The Fir Bolg were strong, led by their hurlers, spearmen of immense strength and agility. They were pitted against the triple goddess Morrigan, who rained down fire and cast great mists and clouds of the darkest night.

Despite the demi-god status of the Tuatha Dé Danann, they were driven back by the Fir Bolg, however their king fell and the indigenous race conceded defeat and took Connaught for their home, leaving the Tuatha Dé Danann the rest of Ireland

.Now around this time, King of the Tuatha Dé Danann, Nuada, lost an arm. Under the doctrine of the Tuatha Dé Danann, no incomplete man was able to reign. Nuada lost not only a limb, but also his crown, which went to Bres, foster son to the Tuatha Dé Danann, but his father was a Fomorian. Bres was a poor leader and showed none of the hospitality and social skills required of a king. While Bres began his reign, Nuada was gifted a silver arm from his physician, Dian Cecht. Miach, the son of Dian Cecht, was impressed by the gift of alchemy shown by his father and studied harder and reaching into darker magic. It was Miach who created living tissue over the silver arm of Nuada, thus enabling him to be restored to power. Was Miach the creator of the first Cyborg? Regardless his work drove his father to jealous rage and filicide.

Incensed by his deposition, Bres sought sanctuary and assistance with retribution from his paternal family, the Fomorians. His grandfather, Balor of the Evil Eye agreed. Balor was so called because he has one eye that would cause death upon his penetrative stare. I often wonder if Balor was the inspiration for the Eye of Sauron, but I digress, the great battle of Magh Tuireadh had begun.

Bres went to war against his former kinsmen, his power in the form of his grandfather. Balor slayed his opponent Nuada with a single gaze from his evil eye. Undeterred at the loss of their King, the

Tuatha Dé Danann were unrelenting in their attack and intent on winning the battle.

The new leader of the Tuatha Dé Danann was brought forth, Lugh, who like Bres, was of Tuatha Dé Danann and Formorian birth. His loyalties were firm however, and he killed his grandfather Balor with a single slingshot into his eye of poison.

Lugh found his half-brother Bres, unprotected on the battlefield. Weak and defenseless, Bres begged for both mercy and his very life. In a moment of pity for his kin, Lugh agreed in exchange for Bres teaching the Formorian people agriculture.

It is interesting to note, that King Nuada had previously rejected Lugh, who had travelled far to the Court of Tara to be accepted as one of the Tuatha Dé Danann. When Lugh had asked for a place as either a blacksmith, wheelwright, swordsman, king's champion, druid, magician, craftsman or wordsmith he was refused. It was only because he excelled at all that he was accepted.

Lugh's power and influence went on to the creation of the festival of Lughnasadh, a Druid festival held on 1 August every year. Such were his strengths and abilities; a test in the form of games was set up in his mother's name that became known as the Tailteann games. These have progressed over recent centuries to become known as the Gaelic Games, played throughout Ireland to this day, growing stronger in popularity every year.

So what became of the Formorians, the Tuatha Dé Danann and even the Fir Bolg? Well we are talking demi-gods, supernatural races and magic – they may have been driven underground, back to the ethereal world of the *Sidhe*, however they are not truly gone. Maybe there will be a third battle and the wars of Magh Tuireadh are not yet over. We will just have to wait and see...

WELCOME TO TIR NA NÓG - THE LAND OF ETERNAL YOUTH

Every self-respecting Irish man or woman knows the story of Tir na nÓg. Often simplified and romanticized as the 'Land of Eternal Youth', this island is believed to be the home of the demi-god race known as the Tuatha Dé Danann. The origins and location of this enigmatic island remain as mysterious as ever. So how did Tir na nÓg become the sanctuary of a lost race of warriors and where is it now?

The Tuatha Dé Danann

As the more cultured of the races of ancient Ireland, their diplomacy and education meant they frequently had the upper hand over rivals such as the Fir Bolg and arch nemeses, the Formorians. All this was set to change however, with the arrival of the Milesians.

The Milesians waged into a fearsome battle against the Tuatha Dé Danann and they were never going to settle until they had complete and utter domination over their rivals. Being the civilized nation they were, the Tuatha did everything they could to negotiate and seek peace and harmonious accord.

With no truce in sight the Tuatha did everything in their power to keep their stronghold, including invoking a mystical tempest to destroy the enemy. The crafty Milesians called upon a daughter of the Tuatha, the goddess Eriu and claimed the land of Eire as their own.

What happened next to the Tuatha Dé Danann is a matter of speculation; however, the outcome was always the same. A land of their own outside of space and time.

Regardless of how they got there, it goes without question that the Tuatha went underground. And this is where it gets interesting.

Tir na nÓg

Think Lord of the Rings and the Undying Lands but do remember which came first. Tir na nÓg is a land of beauty, natural abundance and first and foremost, immortality. Where it is – well that's another question altogether.

Generally, it is thought to lie on the Wild Atlantic Way, off the west coast of Ireland, somewhere beyond the Aran Islands. It has to be remembered, however, that it is a place made of mystical energy and its location is intangible.

Historical records show a Dutch navigator, who settled in Dublin in the 17th century, recorded seeing an island much described as Tir na nÓg. He sighted it off the coast of Greenland, which is some 1500 miles from the Aran Islands.

The island that appeared was protected by potent witchcraft and anyone trying to approach was pushed off course by powerful tempests and drowned at sea. Terrified to meet the same fate, the intrepid explorer made a full turn and headed south only to find the same island emerging on the horizon once again.

The terrain itself is a veritable landscape of waterfalls, mountains, forests and lakes. If you took the most beautiful and awe inspiring Irish vistas they would not hold a candle to what awaits in the land of the *Sidhe*.

Manannán Mac Lir

Manannán mac Lir is the Irish sea god and protector of Tir na nÓg. Much like Poseidon and Hades, his guardianship means the Land of Eternal Youth is well protected from unwanted visitors and the Merrow folk will raise the warning if anyone dares to cross the oceanic boundaries. If Manannán mac Lir permits, every seven years a fortunate few will be blessed to see the land of Tir na nÓg emerge from above the waves.

Reaching the Land of the Tuatha Dé Danann

Legend says the goddess Danu assisted in the escape of the cultured race by hiding them beneath the mounds of the earth, otherwise known as *Sidh*s, and disguising their location with magic. These *Sidh*s were portals and the Tuatha Dé Danann became known as '*Aes Sidh*' or 'people under the mound.' Today that translates as '*Sidhe*' or 'faeries.'

As well as via coastal trickery, Tir na nÓg can be reached through one of the many magical faery portals dotted around the Emerald Isle. In fact, there is one not ten miles from my door called Knockfierna, which translates as the 'Mountain of Truth.'

At certain times of the year such as Samhain, the veil separating ourselves from the Otherworld is at is thinnest and that is when access becomes possible. Remember though, all that glitters *is* most definitely not gold.

Oisín and Tir na nÓg

Oisín was a formidable warrior, one of the Fianna and the son of the legendary Fionn mac Cumhaill. What I should have mentioned is that the *Sidhe* were a devious lot, in particular the '*A Leannan Sidh*,' or faery sweetheart. She is known for luring unsuspecting male humans to Tir na nÓg, with them never to return home.

In this instance Niamh, daughter of Manannán mac Lir, failed in her mission. Whilst Oisín had fallen in love with his femme fatale, she in turn had fallen in love with the greatest poet Ireland had ever known. Niamh carried him back to her land and they lived blissfully together. Time was an unknown quantity to those residing in Tir na nÓg and Oisín was shocked to find three hundred years had passed.

Desperate to see what was left of his people, Oisín travelled back on a white steed with Niamh's blessing. Her only warning was that he should not touch the land of humans, for that would be his demise, as mortality would take hold.

On arrival, Oisín was devastated to discover all that he had held dear was gone. Miserable and lonely, he turned his magic horse towards Tir na nÓg. Just before he entered the waves, he saw an old man needing help to move a boulder. Guiding his horse Embarr, he assisted in what would be his last act of kindness.

Oisín fell from his steed and instantly began to age. It is said Saint Patrick found him and before the Fianna warrior died of old age he recounted his tale of Tir na nÓg.

The Land of Eternal Youth has fluid boundaries and magical wards protecting the Tuatha Dé Danann from harm and invasion. They keep themselves to themselves if you leave them be. If. Of course, when the veils between worlds are at their thinnest, you may catch a glimpse of Tir na nÓg. If you are taken by a Leannan *Sidh* and find your way home, just be sure you never set foot on this mortal coil again, because it will be the last thing you ever do.

Fionn Mac Cumhaill, Benandonner and the Giant's Causeway

One of the first mythological tales any young Irish child learns just happens to be Scottish too. Fionn was an Irish giant who was in an ongoing battle with his nemesis across the sea, a Scottish giant by the name of Benandonner who was larger and much more dangerous. Temper rising, Fionn began to break off pieces of the Antrim Coast and throwing them into the sea to build a series of stepping stones across the water to finish off Benandonner.

Fionn learns that Benandonner is coming for him and is terrified so hatches a plan with his wife to scare off the intimidating ogre once and for all. Dressed as an infant, Fionn is tucked up in a crib as the Scottish giant arrives to the house. Benandonner looms over the helpless Oona as she informs him that Fionn is on an errand. Making pancakes, she puts iron into some of the batch. Handing one to Benandonner that contains the iron, he takes a bite and his tooth is broken.

Oona looks on disdainfully and says her husband eats them without any trouble. She then proceeds to feed an untainted pancake to the 'infant' who gobbles it down without a bother. The giant feels the teeth of the 'child' and is bitten for his trouble!

Realising that if this was the offspring of Fionn, his rival must indeed have strength and power beyond anything he could imagine. Benandonner runs back across the Causeway in terror, smashing the hexagonal shaped basalt columns as he went, leaving only that on the coast of Antrim to ensure Fionn did not follow in his wake.

VENGEANCE, DEATH AND INFIDELITY - IRELAND'S SEVEN DARKEST GODDESSES

Searching for a woman's guide to revenge, infidelity, intoxication and death? We need look no further than some of the Irish goddesses for divine inspiration.

The Fury – Triple Goddesses Morrigan, Badb and Nemain

The sisters known as The Fury are the war goddesses the Morrigan, Badb and Macha. They are the goddesses of battle, strife and sovereignty and harbingers of death for those men who crossed their path. The triple deities are most commonly known in the singular as The Morrigan, translated as Phantom Queen.

No corporeal weapons were needed in order for the Morrigan to take her prey. She relied solely on magic and her ability to shapeshift at will. Known primarily for appearing as a crow to those at death's door, the goddess would also take on the guises of a hag where she would scream for the death of enemy troops, an old washerwoman who is seen washing the clothes of those soldiers selected by her to die and a beautiful, seductive young woman.

Sorceress of the Tuatha Dé Danann

Bé Chuille was a sorceress of great regard and was one of the Tuatha Dé Danann, a master race of supernatural powers. Where mortal weapons would not work in battle, Bé Chuille was called upon to use her magic.

When Carman, a vicious witch from Athens attempted to invade Ireland with her three evil sons, using the darkest of magic. Bé Chuille's powers were pivotal in her downfall and death.

Áine – Cursed Stone, Healing and Vengeance

Áine was a daughter of the sea god Manannán. Although known throughout Limerick and Ireland for her healing nature and herbal remedies, there was a dark side to the goddess.

She had a special stone known as Cathair Áine, and any who sat upon it would begin to lose their minds and go insane.

Any who sat on it three times would be lost forever. The beautiful deity had many lovers and they would be consumed by her passion. Áine's vengeful nature however was not to be treated lightly.

Oilill Olum was a King of Munster who raped Áine and she bit off his ear. His surname means 'one eared' and her action was well thought through, as this rendered him incomplete and by law, unable to continue as king.

Intoxicating Medb

Medb *(pronounced Maeve)* was the goddess of intoxication and another warrior goddess. Taking promiscuity to new heights, she would have upwards of twenty or thirty men in one night.

Kings would 'wed' her on their coronation day and complete the ritual by imbibing copious amounts of mead to ensure they would maintain their position of power.

One of Medb's lover's was a virile hero by the name of Fergus mac Roich, who was more than a match for the goddess's sexual appetite. He turned traitor and joined her in the battle of Táin Bó Cúailnge against his fellow Ulstermen. At one point in the height of attack, Medb needed to relieve herself and so urinated behind the shield of Fergus. It was said that three streams were created to form three waterways in order that mills could be built upon them.

The Divine Hag

Cailleach Beare is a crone goddess mostly associated in Ireland with the Beara Peninsula on the South West coast.

Her time of power is from Samhain to Beltane and she is the goddess of winter. She would raise brutal arctic storms, snow and ice and the hag carried a magic staff that turned the greenery she touched to the grey withered death of winter.

Her appearance is hideous and terrifying, blue face, long pointed teeth and filthy, bedraggled hair. As her season ends, she turns into a block of stone until winter returns once more.

Boann – Reluctant River Goddess of the Boyne

With a name that translates as *white cow*, Boann was one of the Tuatha Dé Danann and married to the legendary King Nechtan.

Boann was committing adultery with a god known as Daghdha and so intent was she on keeping it a secret to avoid retribution, when she conceived, the deities made the sun stand still in the sky for nine months, so her son Aengus was born on the same day.

Nechtan was the only person allowed to approach the Well of Wisdom, Connla's Well. Furious that she was forbidden to go where her husband could, Boann stormed to the well and defiantly walked around it anti-clockwise as a mark of disrespect.

The waters surged and gushed out towards the sea, creating the River Boyne in the province of Leinster. Boann herself was violently swept away, losing an arm, a leg and an eye. These injuries proved fatal as her act of petulance cost Boann her life.

Aoibhell and the Deadly Harp

With a name meaning ardour, Aoibhell, guardian of the Dalcassians was always going to be passionate and demanding.

Her place of residence was on a grey rock overlooking the River Shannon, where she would hold regular midnight courts. The defendants would be husbands who were accused of not sexually satisfying their wives and Aoibhell would be judge, jury and executioner.

The goddess appeared to a young couple and in an effort to sway the male lover, offered him two hundred servants of the *Sidhe* in exchange for giving up his mortal woman and laying with Aoibhell. When he refused she disappeared in a sulk.

Aoibhell took a lover called Dubhlaing ua Artigan, a man who had fallen foul of his king. When he was reunited with his clansmen and went to battle, the goddess's demands not to go were ignored. To protect him, Aoibhell wrapped a Druid cloak of invisibility around him, which although effective, led Dubhlaing to be called a coward on the battlefield.

When he tore it off, he was summoned to the furious Aoibhell who commanded he withdrew from fighting and offered him two hundred years of life by her side. He refused to be disloyal, so she informed him his proud blood would spill across the field of war the following day. Both Dubhlaing and his King died.

Aoibhell also played a harp, which would mean imminent death to those who heard it. As the original protector of the O'Brien Clan, she has been the Banshee for all O'Briens ever since.

So, if you ever wondered why Irish women were so strong, passionate and fiery, you need look no further than these compelling female deities – and if you were thinking of crossing one, remember hell hath no fury like a goddess scorned!

GODS OF LIGHT AND DARKNESS – CROM DUBH, LUGHNASA AND SAINT PATRICK

Folklore and traditions of Ireland have always been intertwined with Pagan, Celtic and Christian rituals; however, there is no time more evident of this strange combination of beliefs than this when July ends and August begins. Festivals pertaining to the gods Lugh and Crom Dubh as well as pilgrimages in honour of Saint Patrick have been taking place for centuries.

The common denominators for all of these celebrations and rites are harvest and fertility. Dating back to the earliest accounts of the Fir Bolg and through to recent times, the inhabitants of Ireland would do whatever it took to ensure a bountiful yield and enough produce to sustain them during the dark and unforgiving winter months.

Today, there are several recognised festivals that take place on the last Sunday in July and the first day of August, including the Pagan celebration of Lughnasadh, Crom Dubh Sunday, Garland or Bilberry Sunday and the Reek Sunday Pilgrimage to Croagh Patrick.

All of them have definitive origins and purpose, so let's take a look at them one by one, how they all link together and how they have survived in modern Irish Society.

Crom Dubh – The Sacrificial Fertility God

Crom Dubh is a name that evolved from the Fertility god *Crom Cruaich* and is synonymous with dark practices and folklore. It is believed that as well as the ritual slaughter of bulls in the name of the 'Crooked One', human sacrifices were also offered up to ensure prosperous crops and fat, juicy cattle.

Crom Cruaich was first introduced to Ireland some time before the arrival of the Tuatha Dé Danann, a cultured race of demi-gods. A Milesian known as Tigernmas settled in Ireland and was one of the first of the High Kings. He brought the beginnings of structure to the hierarchy, including a system of coloured clothing, the more dyes, the higher your status. He also introduced idol worship and in particular the worship of the sacrificial god.

The *Book of Leinster* describes the idol as a golden sculpture, surrounded by twelve stone statues. The shrine stood resplendent at the peak of Magh Slécht in County Cavan and was a place of worship for those who idolized the dark god of fertility and sacrifice. It is ironic and quite disconcerting that the King who idolized *Crom Cruaich* and brought him so many followers should die as a result of his actions. King Tigernmas and the vast majority of his troops mysteriously died on Magh Slécht on the night of Samhain, now known as Halloween, as they worshipped their dark, sacrificial deity.

Crom Cruaich was said to have descended into obscurity and his worship ended with the arrival of Saint Patrick. The man who brought Christianity to Ireland stood on a hilltop opposite Magh Slécht and cast out his staff known as Bachal Isu, across to the Idol of *Crom Cruaich*, causing it to tumble and the twelve surrounding stones were devoured by the Irish landscape.

Crom Dubh descended from *Crom Cruaich* and became more of a worshipped figure of mythology than a god. The practice of *Crom Dubh* Sunday, the last Sunday in July continued down through the centuries however, with gifts of crops and produce taken to the hillside and offered to the fallen dark one. The practice is still continued in some more rural and mountainous regions of Ireland.

The darkest incarnation of the sacrificial god *Crom Cruaich* however, is the Dullahan, also known as *Gan Ceann*, meaning without a head. The creature hunts the souls of the dying in the night. The god did not want to be denied human souls following the introduction of Christianity and so disguised himself as the one without a head, a tribute to the sacrifices through decapitation that gave *Crom Dubh* his power.

Lugh of the Tuatha Dé Danann

Lugh was not only one of Ireland's early high kings, but a demi-god. His father was of the Tuatha Dé Danann and his mother was of the Formorian race, supernatural beings who celebrated chaos and wildness. The couple's marriage was forged through the need for a coalition and Lugh was born. As he grew older, Lugh joined with King Nuada of the Tuatha Dé Danann to defeat the Formorians and their evil leader Balor, during the Second Battle of Magh Tuireadh at Tara.

Once Lugh had slain Balor with a single slingshot to his evil eye of death, Bres turned to his traitor kin Bres who was alone, weak and injured on the field of battle and Bres began to beg for his life. Although highly intelligent and gifted, the Tuatha Dé Danann were unskilled in agriculture. At his point of victory, Lugh forced King Bres to promise to teach his people how to farm the lands in return for mercy.

Lugh's foster mother was Tailtiu, a fertility goddess who died of exhaustion after clearing the rugged and barren landscape and preparing the fields of Ireland for the sowing of crop. Upon her death the Aonach, a congress brought together on the death of royalty, was convened and funeral traditions commenced.

Tailteann Games and the First Festival of Lughnasadh

As was the way with previous funeral gatherings, it was a place for games, remembrance, celebration and the proclaiming of new laws.

The funeral pyre was lit, mourning songs and chanting began and the first Tailteann Games took place in honour of Lugh's foster mother in the place now known as Teltown in County Meath. As a testament to both the Tuatha Dé Danann and Formorians, as well as Lugh's own strengths as both a warrior and master craftsman, the games were contests in both physical and mental agility.

Competitions for physical prowess included athletics, sword fighting, archery, horseracing and swimming, while other challenges were in the Arts. Storytelling, song and dance were of high importance and awards went to the best smiths, weavers and armourers of the day.

From the time of the first festival, new laws were passed. One such law was the Brehon Law for marriage. On the day of Lughnasadh, there would be a mass wedding among clans and that marriage would stand good for one year and one day, after which time it could be nullified if either party so wished.

As the celebration of Lughnasadh continued through the generations, the first cutting of the corn would be offered in tribute to Lugh, laid upon the highest piece of ground, a tradition that was previously reserved for *Crom Dubh*. As with so many Irish practices, they are not let go of lightly and the sacrifice of an aged bull would take place, a remnant of the worship to the fallen but not forgotten 'Crooked One'.

Bilberry Sunday

During the early Lughnasadh celebrations, Bilberries would be consumed at every mealtime, as the festival tied in with the harvest time for this blueberry like fruit.

This common practice evolved into its own ritual known as Bilberry Sunday. On the last Sunday in June for generations, the young men and women of rural Ireland would climb into the mountainous areas and pick the bilberries from the heather clad and rocky terrain. It was a painstaking and long process, so during the hours of work it became common for the single ones to pair off, matches made and courtship begun.

Reek Sunday and Saint Patrick

The practice of climbing to hilltops during the worship of *Crom Dubh*, then Lugh evolved further with the spreading of Christianity throughout Ireland.

Reek Sunday takes place on the last Sunday in July and is the day that dedicated Christians climb to the top of Croagh Patrick in County Mayo, many clambering barefoot over the rocky hillside to the summit, some two and a half thousand feet high in homage to Saint Patrick and to prove their commitment to their faith.

As is typical of all of Ireland's Christian traditions it evolved from and is firmly intertwined with Pagan and Celtic practice. For centuries it was a place of Pagan Pilgrimage and would have been the site of the placing of the corn and sacrifice for both *Crom Cruaich* and Lugh, however due to its associations with Ireland's Patron Saint, it has become the focal point of the Catholic year in Ireland, even though it falls at Lughnasadh, a distinctly Pagan celebration.

While the focal point of worship and ritual may have changed over the centuries, in an agricultural and fertile land the purpose remains the same – to pray for good health, fertile lands and a bountiful harvest for the winter months and of course to give thanks.

It has become clear that regardless of Christianity, the teachings of Saint Patrick and the move away from rituals and traditions of any kind in a busy and commercially driven Irish Society, the Pagan and Celtic elements of our heritage remain and will never be forgotten.

Newgrange: A Winter Solstice Tale

Newgrange is a historical monument that stands within the Boyne Valley in County Meath and is over 5000 years old. Older than Stonehenge and the Great Pyramids of Giza, it is classified as a Passage Tomb but is better described as an Ancient Temple. A construction of astrological, spiritual, religious and ceremonial importance, Newgrange remains as one of the world's most significant heritage sites.

The main structure is formed in a mound over one acre and has a retaining wall of some 97 kerbstones, richly decorated in Megalithic art. It is part of a series of structures built along a meandering part of the River Boyne known as the Neolithic Brú na Bóinne complex.

During medieval times, Newgrange and the surrounding constructions were introduced into folklore as many believed that the ancient Kings of Tara were interred here, whilst others thought it as the home of the mythical God like beings known as Tuatha De Danann. In fact, texts from the 11th and 12th centuries give accounts of residency and clan deceit relating to the Brú na Bóinne.

During this time, the mounds and surrounding land had become a part of the holdings of the Cistercian Abbey of Mellifont. These farms were known as granges and by the late 1300s, the site was known as 'the new grange'.

The 19-metre-long inner passage leads to a cruciform chamber, so called because the overall layout represents a cross.

Archaeological digs inside the passage have produced burnt and decayed human bone, which gives credence to the belief that corpses were placed within Newgrange, some having been cremated as was customary. Artefacts including tools and jewellery were also found during excavation in a manner similar to other Neolithic Irish passage graves.

Newgrange is of course most famous for the incredible event within the passage and chamber that takes place during the Winter Solstice. At approximately 9 am on the 21st of December, as the sun rises, a narrow ray of light begins to penetrate an orifice above the entrance of the passage known as the roof-box. As the sun ascends over a period of some fourteen minutes, the beam of sunlight travels along the passageway, widening until it reaches the central chamber. The entire room is spectacularly illuminated, marking a significant astronomical moment in the calendar. A major feat of Neolithic engineering to welcome in a new year that has remained virtually unchanged in thousands of years. So coveted are the few spaces available to witness this historical and magical event, a lottery is held each year. Subject to weather conditions, the lucky chosen few wait in anticipation in the dark hollow before spending fourteen minutes of wonder and excitement, watching as the ray of sun creeps towards the sleeping chamber. They are witnesses to a bygone age of mystery and ingenuity until Newgrange is once again plunged into darkness for another year.

Beltane - A May Celebration of Fire, Flowers and Fertility

Despite Christianity coming to Ireland's shores in the 5th century, rural Ireland has never let go of her Pagan ceremonies, superstitions and belief in the prevalent spirit realm and faeries. As a part of this way of life, certain times of the year are deemed the most powerful and are to be recognized as such by way of protection and prosperity rituals, with Beltane being no exception.

Beltane, or '*Bealtaine*' as it is known in Ireland, marks the start of summer, halfway between the Spring Equinox and Summer Solstice and translates as 'Bright Fire'. As is true with all Celtic festivals, Beltane is celebrated in alignment with the heavens and the moving of the seasons, with the last day of April or the first of May usually selected as the official day to light the Beltane fires and so begin the customary rites of the season.

The most notable Beltane Fire in Ireland was lit on the Hill of Uisneach in the County of Westmeath, known as the mystical navel of Ireland. Cattle would be driven between two Beltane fires as part of a purifying ritual to safeguard the herd and families would take home embers to light their own hearth fires for continued protection. In the event you were to remove an ignited piece of turf from a house, you would remove the blessing of the home and doom the family to bad luck.

The fires were merely the beginning however. In nature as spring is very much the mating period and a time for birth, many of the rituals were fuelled with sexual energy in an effort to increase fertility among the clans. An effigy of a woman known as the May Baby would be attached to the Maypole, a phallic symbol. The effigy would be covered in the flowers of the season as well as straw and ribbons, while a male and female of the community would dress up and dance around the Maypole in a crude and lurid manner. These displays of vulgarity were believed to increase fertility and help those who were trying to conceive.

As with Samhain, Beltane was of vital importance to the farming communities of Ireland and the practices accompanying the festival were reflective of this fact. In earlier times, cattle would be herded to the nearest fairy fort and the blood of the livestock would be spilled in order to appease the spirits, while
Hawthorn and Rowan twigs were across the horns of the herd to prevent milk thieves, as the right curse could cause an entire summer's milk to be stolen from the cows.

Herbs were gathered on the first day of May, and boiled with hair from a cow's tail. It would be carefully preserved, with a small amount being placed inside the churn and inside of the pails before milking and churning commenced. This was believed to guard against disease and ensure a healthy production of dairy produce for the season. Of course, if you wanted to ensure the demise of your neighbour's farm, you would cast a malevolent curse by placing three grains of corn into balls of yellow clay and position in each corner of their field.

Switches and brooms were made and stocked before May, as any put together during this month would bring further bad luck, and milk was poured across the threshold to keep out the faeries. The May Bush or May Bough was created from the branch or part of a Rowan or Hawthorn tree, placed outside the house and decorated with rags and ribbons. This would ward off evil spirits, mischievous faery folk and bring a good harvest to the homestead. The task of adorning the May Bush was often given to the children to keep them occupied and out of the clutches of the faeries!

The gathering of May Flowers was also of great importance and a task that once again fell to the children of the community. Posies would be put together and placed in front of homes, on cattle and in wells for protection and good fortune.

Perhaps the most permanent reminder of the festival of Beltane is the ancient Beltany Stone Circle in Donegal. As the name suggests, it is believed this circle of stones was the site of the celebration of Beltane. The central stone is the only one to be decorated and faces towards the hill known as Tullyrap. On May Day, the sun rises above the hill in alignment with the circle and appears from behind the decorative stone, a sign of renewed energy, vitality and promise for the summer.

So whether you are gathering flowers, dancing around a Maypole or lighting a Beltane fire, you are wished good luck and all the blessings of Beltane – and remember to keep an eye on infants born on this May Day, as they are believed to possess the power to see the faery folk!

Samhain, Superstition and Suppers for the Dead

As Samhain draws to a close for another year, it is a time to reflect on the origins of this pagan celebration and what it meant to those who, over centuries maintained the traditions and rites synonymous with this feast in Ireland.

Samhain (*pronounced Sow-en*) began at sunset on the 31st of October and end at sunset on the 1st of November, signalling the beginning of a new year. It is one of four major celebrations during the Celtic year and signifies the end of summer. This was a time were cattle were brought in and slaughtered for the winter months, the bitter cold and poor pasture leaving farmers no choice.

The ceremonies for Samhain were intertwined - the light and dark, protections against bad spirits and misfortune and a welcome for the dead to return.

As with Beltane, at the heart of Samhain is the customary communal bonfire. The fire was a protection ritual, to purge bad fortune and influence and to defend from harm during the long hard winter.

All house fires would be quenched, the central fire the only one alight. Each family would take a burning ember from the bonfire, carried in a hollowed-out turnip and use it to reignite their own hearth, instilling the same protection and cleansing into their own homes and lives.

The bones of slaughtered cattle were onto the fire as an offering for a good winter and objects symbolizing wishes or ailments would be thrown on the flames, individuals hoping to be cured or receive their hearts desires.

Samhain is the time of year when the curtain between our world and the next becomes so fragile that the both the fairies and the dead can take a simple step between realms.

Many of the dead were welcomed back into the family fold with open arms, a place set for returning souls to sit at the table. This was known as a Dumb Supper and all living guests were to dine in silence, listening and watching for a word or sign from their dearly departed.

The fear for celebrants was that of course malevolent spirits could also cross over as could the Devil himself. These evil entities were thought to wreak havoc on the villages by making cattle sick and bringing disease to households so 'guising' would be carried out as a symbolic gesture to hide from those not wanted.

A typical costume was the *Láir Bhán* (White Mare) which would consist of a man covered in a white cloth, carrying a horse's skull in his hands. He would lead a group of youths from farm to farm blowing on cow horns and asking for food. Woe betide any farmer who refused for he would be cursed with bad luck for the coming year.

As well as the dead, homeowners had to contend with the fairies travelling abroad to create mischief on this most ethereal of nights. Gifts in the form of food or milk would be left on doorsteps to guarantee a fairy blessing. Anyone foolish enough to not do so were subject to pranks by the cheeky wee folk at best and victim to a fairy curse at worst.

It was these beliefs and traditions that led us to trick or treating and costumes in today's Halloween, so a fistful of sweets for protection from mischief and misfortune is a small price to pay don't you think?

Wren's Day

'The wran, the wran, the king of all birds,
On St. Stephen's day was caught in the furze.
His body is little but his family is great
So rise up landlady and give us a trate.
And if your trate be of the best
Your soul in heaven can find its rest.
And if your trate be of the small
It won't plaze the boys at all.
A glass of whiskey and a bottle of beer
Merry Christmas and a glad New Year.
So up with the kettle and down with the pan
And give us a penny to bury the wran.

Although there are many variations of the infamous Wren Boys' song, these particular words are the ones I recall being sang to me by my mother at Christmas time. The history of the Wren Boys and Wren's Day is a long and complex one with a myriad of potential meanings and beginnings. It must be said, however, that the tradition itself is very much a stalwart of the Irish Christmas and one that is still very much a part of St, Stephen's Day celebrations today.

What Are Wren Boys And Wren's Day?

Wren's Day or *Lá an Dreoilín* can be dated back in one form or another to the second century and probably started in connection with Samhain as opposed to Christmas. Usually found in rural areas, this tradition and celebration centres around the wren, an iconic bird in Irish Mythology and Pagan and Christian religions. On St. Stephen's Day, boys used to dress up in brightly coloured clothes and were known as the Wren Boys. Others would dress in suits made from straw and be known as 'mummers'.

Until the early 20th century, a real wren would be hunted and placed in a makeshift cage at the top of a pole that would be carried by the Wren leader. The challenge in the hunt of course is that the wren is scarce in winter! The Wren Boys and the Mummers would march through small townlands and villages, demanding money to keep the bird alive. At the end of the day the money was used to throw a celebratory gathering for the townsfolk. The boys were by musicians and would hand out feathers to those who donated for good luck.

The pole would take centre stage at the celebrations, being bedecked in ribbons, evergreens and flowers and the locals would dance around it. As times began to change, the real wren was replaced with a fake bird that would be hidden for the Wren Boys and Mummers to find as opposed to hunting the wren.

Why the Wren?

Celtic Mythology

Clíodhna was a Celtic goddess of feasting and hunting, with her home in Munster and was believed to be the original Banshee. Whilst Clíodhna had a regal reputation and was worshipped, she also had a sinister side. She would lure men through her beauty and powers of seduction and they would drown off the coast of Cork, where she resided. Finally, one man discovered her secrets of magic and power and devised a way to destroy her. Realising this, Clíodhna transfigured into a wren and made her escape back to the Other Realm.

Druids

For centuries, those who practice Paganism have revered the wren and viewed it as a symbol of divinity and wisdom. The wren was considered so precious by the Druids, that curses were cast upon those who sought to steal eggs or hatchlings, leaving homes destroyed and bodies mutilated. The wren would also be used in the Pagan practice of Divination, each chirp and sound deemed a message for the Druid High Priests. Indeed, the Irish word for wren, *Dreoilín*, translates as 'Druid Bird' and as Samhain approached, the wren was a symbol of the old year and the robin a celebration of the new.

Christianity and Saint Stephen

Although Saint Stephen was not Irish, he became a patron saint and the subject of an Irish National Holiday. One of the original deacons selected by the Apostles, Saint Stephen was outspoken with his teachings and distaste for the hypocrisy of the Jewish Authorities. A warrant was issued for his arrest and while in hiding, it is said that a wren gave away his location by chattering and flapping its wings. Stephen was captured and stoned to death, making him the first official martyr of Christianity.

It was these events that enabled the Christian Clerics in Ireland in the Dark Ages to convince people to turn against Paganism, citing the wren as a symbol of evil.

The Wren of Treason

There are two events in Irish history where the wren is said to have caused the demise of Irish forces. Once during the Viking invasion, Irish soldiers had an opportunity to stage an attack as the enemy slept. A single wren landed on the drum of a soldier and began pecking at crumbs, creating a cacophony that awoke the Vikings and led to the slaughter of the home forces. The very same turn of events occurred centuries later during a planned ambush on Cromwellian troops.

The Wren in Modern Ireland

As with most Irish Folklore and Tradition, the origins are an entwining of Christianity, Paganism and Celtic Mythology, so the definitive meaning of the wren and Wren's Day will never be truly known. The practice continues however, in small towns and particularly parts of Sligo, Leitrim and Kerry, with Dingle having an extraordinary display of costume and colour every St. Stephen's Day and in prior years would put on a display of early combat.

The Wrens and Mummers now consist of men, women and children and the focus is very much on traditional music, with the Wrens travelling between pubs and collecting money for charity and performing in retirement homes and hospitals.

Brigid – Goddess to Saint, the Cross and the Feast of Imbolc

When first day of February is upon us, the instantly recognisable cross of St. Brigid is appearing everywhere in honour of her feast day. So how did the Irish pagan festival of Imbolc and the goddess of Fire lead to the story of St. Brigid with one of the most recognisable crosses in the world?

Brigid the Goddess

The deity Brigid was said to have been born at dawn's first light with a crown of fire glowing from her head. One of the supernatural race of the gifted known as the Tuatha Dé Danann, she was the goddess of the Spring, arts, crafts, poetry, medicine and the humble smith.

Her name came from the old Irish *Breo saighit* meaning fiery arrow and where Brigid walked flowers and shamrocks grew and she radiated inspiration, knowledge and healing with the light that surrounded her.

Brigid married Bres, a king of the Tuatha Dé Danann but one at war with her own clan. It was hoped their marriage would calm the tension between the warring families, however hostilities just increased.

Her son Ruandan lost his life in battle and so distraught was Brigid that as she sang and wept over her son's body, her harmonic cries heard throughout the length and breadth of Ireland and so began the tradition of keening at the wakes of the dead.

Brigid then became devoted to healing and, following the death of her child, became the protector of children and childbirth. Her shrine was created by an ancient druid oak in Kildare that was so sacred. No weapon could be brought into it. Her priestesses took care of her perpetual flame, the sacred fire of Brigid, one each day for nineteen days and on the twentieth day Brigid herself would attend the flame.

Imbolc

This pagan festival marks the beginning of Spring and is at the start of February, midway between the winter solstice and the spring equinox. The meaning is said to have come from the old Irish meaning *'In the belly'*. It has been documented in detail in the earliest of Irish Literature and is affiliated with the goddess Brigid.

Brigid was said to visit homes at this time and a bed would be made and food and drink laid out to welcome her and invite her blessings. Items of clothing would also be laid out to receive her divine touch. Like the other festivals, the date of Imbolc pertains to the alignment of megalithic monuments with the sun such as the Mound of Hostages on Tara.

Feasts were had, and fires lit as a part of the celebration and divination of Imbolc. Candles and fires were lit in recognition of Brigid's perpetual light and it was a time to look for portents of the future.

The wells of the goddess were circled in the direction of the sun as prayers were given for good health. The water was then taken for livestock, family and to bless the home.

Brigid the Saint

Brigid was said to have lived from the mid-fifth to the early sixth century, born into a druid family. Her mother was converted to Christianity by St. Patrick himself and young Brigid was reared on the milk of a cow that appeared to her, a story also told in respect of Brigid the Goddess.

Brigid was a blessed and religious child, so it was no surprise that she pledged her life to God and began her path of healing. After receiving the veil from St. Macaille, she went to Kildare and built a monastery for the monks and one for her nuns, becoming the first Abbess of Ireland in the late 5th century.

It is said that she chose this place to follow on the work of the goddess, taking on the perpetual flame as a symbol of the light of new Christianity, which was still so alien to the Irish.

In another nod to the fire goddess, St. Brigid founded a School of Art specialising in metalwork and illumination, from which came some of the most impressive work of the time including the legendary Book of Kildare.

Brigid was revered largely due to her work with the poor and the sick, particularly women and this in turn lead to her veneration and sainthood. There are wells throughout Ireland known as Brigid's wells and the waters are said to be miraculous and promote healing and good health. Pilgrimages take place to each of these shrines and they are as relevant today as they ever were.

Brigid's Cross

It is thought that the cross itself was a symbol that far pre-dated Christianity and belonged to pagan protection rites. That said, the story of the rush cross relating to St. Brigid is the one carried forward through the centuries.

Brigid was sat at the bedside of a dying chieftain and she distracted him by making a cross from rushes that lay nearby. When she explained the meaning of the cross, the chieftain was said to have seen the light and was baptised there on his deathbed.

Today there are workshops and gatherings of folk who come together to make the rush cross in honour of St. Brigid and her feast day on 1st February and there are even on-line tutorial videos to teach you how to make them!

There is no question that the legend of Brigid the goddess and the life of Brigid the Saint became inextricably intertwined from early medieval times and to this day, it remains that way. Whether you believe in Brigid the goddess, Brigid the saint or indeed both, the message of creativity, healing and new life is the same, leaving the darkness behind as we move forward into the sun.

DEATH, SUPERSTITION AND CURSES

Celtic Harbingers of Death

Many a conversation in Ireland starts with 'do you know who's dead?' Death is a normal topic of discussion any self-respecting Seanchái (Irish Storyteller) will include death and haunting in his tale. In modern day, Ireland, the customs of old still remain and the event is treated with weighted respect and tradition. We seem to have a fascination and fear of our own mortal demise, which stems back to our ancient roots and the safeguarding of the soul.

For the majority, it isn't so much the dread of death itself, but what happens to the spirit and where it goes afterwards. There have always been the takers of souls in the form of demons, fairies, spirits and other ethereal beings. Over the centuries, the Irish have got wise and found different ways to repel or hide from those looking to reap the soul and cast it to eternal damnation – or worse.

To find the right protection from these creatures of darkness, you have to know who they are and what they want. Some are merely harbingers; others seek to harvest your very essence of being. Those such as the Banshee will (mostly) just warn you that death is imminent; however, there are two terrifying beings you should avoid at all costs.

Sluagh

Once thought to be Angels that have tumbled from the grace of God, the *Sluagh Sidhe* actually have far more sinister origins and purpose. Can you imagine how evil you have to be, that your soul is deemed too tainted for the fires of Hades and you are rejected by Satan himself? Well that is who the *Sluagh* are – souls of sinners not wanted by Heaven or Hell, destined to roam the Earth and take the departed for no reason other than the thrill of the hunt and to add to their ever-growing number.

Unlike other *Sidhe*, the *Sluagh* are unable to walk this mortal coil. They ride on the wind as a host, unable to touch the ground. They travel as a flock and to all intents and purposes look like a conspiracy of ravens, which is probably one of the reasons the raven is seen as a portent of death. As the howling wind and darkening sky take hold, they close in and it is clear they are not bird like at all. With wizened, leathery wings and gnarled, skeletal frames, these twisted creatures fly in from the west and seek out the homes of the dying. This is why one of the traditions that still holds today is to close any westerly facing windows when a loved one is taking a last breath.

Sadly, not every innocent (or indeed not so innocent) soul escapes the clutches of the evil *Sluagh* and these misfortunes are caught up in the host of the soul hunters, not to touch the Earth again or reach Heaven or Hell for all eternity.

The Dullahan

The Dullahan, and before him ,, *Crom Dubh*, are descended from the god *Crom Cruaich* and are synonymous with dark rituals, death and folklore.

Crom Cruaich was first introduced to Ireland some time before the arrival of the Tuatha Dé Danann. Tigernmas was one of the first High Kings of Ireland and as a Milesian brought the worship of this deathly idol to Ireland, building a shrine at the top of Magh Slécht in County Cavan in order to win favour from his god.

King Tigernmas and most of his troops mysteriously died on Magh Slécht on the night of Samhain, now known as Halloween, as they worshipped their dark, sacrificial deity. As the centuries passed, *Crom Dubh* evolved from *Crom Cruaich* and became a worshipped figure in his own right. He is still left 'offerings' in rural parts of Ireland today on *Crom Dubh* Sunday.

The darkest incarnation of the sacrificial god however, is the Dullahan, also known as *Gan Ceann*, meaning without a head. *Crom Dubh* did not want to be denied human souls following the introduction of Christianity and so disguised himself as the one without a head, a tribute to the sacrifices by beheading that gave *Crom Cruaich/Dubh* his power.

For centuries, the Celts have believed the head to be incredibly powerful, both the sacred and physical resting place of the soul. Warriors would decapitate their foes and keep them to ward off evil and gain more power. Those believed to have died as deviants would have stones placed in their mouths to stop the evil soul escaping. It is no surprise therefore, that one of Ireland's most feared unearthly beings incorporates all of the Celtic beliefs over the ages. *Gan Ceann* is a part of the 'Unseelie court' of the fairy realm, filled with the nastiest and darkest of the *Sidhe* and his job is to reap your soul. He carries his head in the crook of his arm, black eyes darting from the mottled, decaying flesh stretched thinly across his skull, searching for his prey.

The Dullahan carries a whip made from the spine of a human corpse as he stands on his wagon. The wheel spokes are made of thighbone and covered with dried human skin and a jet-black horse with eyes of glowing embers pulls the wagon.

The headless horseman has supernatural vision, and when he senses a soul for the taking, he holds his head high, seeing across landscapes, through windows and into the darkest corners of the most remote homes.

The soul taker does not stop for anyone and all locks swing open, so no one is safe. If you get in his way, at best your eyes will be lashed out with his whip or the Dullahan will throw a bowl of human blood upon you. The stain cannot be removed, and you are marked as his next target.

Certain festivals increase the power of The Dullahan and this is a time to stay in and draw your curtains tightly. If you are out in the still of night, there is no protection from this agent of death. He does however fear one thing – gold. Throwing a piece in his path may make him back off for a while and may be the only thing that will save you.

The Dullahan is only permitted to speak once on each ride and that is to utter the name of the person who is going to die. When he finds his quarry and speaks their name aloud, their spirit is brought forth to be devoured.

Banshee

Banshees have forever been known as portents of death; however, there have been sightings of these wailing spirits seeking death for revenge and torment.

This evil being has the appearance of a wretched old hag, dress shredded, matted grey hair, pointed rotting teeth and long, yellow fingernails. If she sets her mind to have you as her prey, she will stalk you, forcing you to listen to her soul-wrenching scream of despair until you go insane and your own soul is lost in the depths of her evil cry. If you are lucky, you will have a quick death by looking into her blood red eyes, filled with enough loathing and agony to kill you instantly. For those who have been strong enough not to succumb to either? She will rip you to death with her bare hands.

The Foxes of Gormonston

In Irish Peerage the title of Baron or Viscount of Gormonston belongs to the patriarch of the Preston family and has been around since the late fourteenth century, their residence being Gormonston Castle in Drogheda, County Meath.

The Castle remained in the family until the 1950s, when it was sold to a Holy Order to create a school. Prior to that however, it was the location of one of the strangest occurrences for generations. With the first instance reported in the seventeenth century, it was documented that the foxes in the surrounding countryside would know when the head of the Preston household was dying, even if that fact was unbeknown to the family themselves.

Arriving in twos and amassing under the window of the Viscount's bedchamber, the foxes would howl and cry all night long. Servants would do their utmost to drive the animals away, only for them to return to their place of vigil. Once the Viscount had passed away, the foxes soundlessly faded into the night.

Hellhounds

Shucks, or Devil Dogs, have long been written about in Irish history. They are black as the night, large, with glowing red eyes, some with cloven hooves instead of paws. Sometimes they are raised to protect treasure such as the one that breathes fire at Castle Biggs in Tipperary, others simply to forewarn of death.

Quite possibly the inspiration for Sherlock Holmes and the Hound of the Baskervilles, they are seen in rural and isolated areas, although once your eyes set on the Shuck the mark of death is upon you.

In Kanturk, County Cork a local man by the name of Foley was walking home when he encountered the hell beast on the road, eyes glowing and snarling. He stood terrified as the Shuck brushed up against his leg. Unable to sleep that night, he told his family of his encounter and died just a few days later.

Ornithomancy

Crows and Ravens have long been emblematic of death, made even more foreboding by their predisposition to feed on carrion, the decaying flesh of animals, as well as their black plumage. These birds were purported to be chaperones, guiding the souls of the departed into the next world as well as conduits between this world and the spirit plain.

In Ireland, there are references going back to ancient times and in Celtic folklore, The Morrigan is symbolised by a crow. She is a goddess of battle, strife and sovereignty and a harbinger of doom for those men who cross her path.

No corporeal weapons were needed for the Morrigan to take her prey. She relied solely on magic and her ability to shapeshift at will and is known primarily for appearing as a crow to those at death's door.

The belief has continued over the centuries that when a single raven or crow has appeared at a house, tapping on the window, a death within was looming.

In the late eighteenth century there is an account of the Ross-Lewin family in Kilchrist, in County Clare being terrorised by their own messenger of death. The father of the household was away on business and his children went to spend the evening with friends. On returning home, they passed the old abandoned church where they saw an old hag crying and waving her hands in the air.

Thinking her crazy, the terrified youths went towards her only for the old woman to vanish. They sped home and told their mother of their encounter and the matriarch expressed her fears of a death in the family. At that moment, an enormous raven landed on the windowsill and tapped three times on the pane. A few days later, the family were in mourning as news reached them of the death of Mr Ross-Lewin.

Birds of ill news do not end there. Thrushes flying in the window and settling, and white owls seen during the day are also signs of a bereavement in the home.

Irish Funeral Traditions

The Irish are known for their religious beliefs, superstitions and celebration of life and these traits are reflected in death. Every care is taken to ensure a smooth journey for loved ones into heaven and to keep the Gates of Hell firmly shut.

The Sin Eater

Sin Eating may be known to various cultures, however in Ireland it was practiced up until the late 19th century. Sin Eaters were called upon by households that had suffered bereavement in an effort to avoid damnation and save the souls of the dearly departed. Considered to be the lowest of professions, the task usually fell to a disgraced priest ex-communicated from the Church, who would travel from village to village visiting the homes of the deceased, charging for his services. Instead of absolving the dead from their transgressions, he would take food and drink as part of a spiritual cleansing ritual in which blood would pass onto the food and he would effectively 'eat' the sins, allowing the soul of the dead to pass into Heaven and rest in peace. When a Sin Eater died however, he would enter into the pits of Hell, carrying the weight of all those sins he had ingested for eternity.

Keening

Many families in Ireland for generations have had their own Banshee (*Bean Sidhe*) tied to their mortality who lets out a blood curdling scream when death in the house is imminent. Not to be outdone, families without such an entity would hire a professional Keener (from the Irish *Caoineadh*, meaning to cry) to do the job instead. These were not random wails from mourners but controlled high-pitched lamentations from trained women who would seek payment in food and drink. The Keeners would attend the wake to perform and not a moment sooner. In the event keening began before the dead had been laid out, evil spirits would be invoked, and the Hounds of Hell were believed to be sent to collect the soul of the departed and take it back to eternal torment.

Waking

Being Ireland, there has always been a fondness for a drop of Guinness. Legend has it that waking began as this tasty beverage was supped from pewter tankards and the side effect was lead poisoning. This caused the consumer to take on the appearance of being dead, when in fact they were in a catatonic state. Family and friends would therefore stand vigil to see if they would wake to avoid the horror of being buried alive. The tankard story is believed to be a myth and the truth is that Waking has been a Celtic tradition for centuries as a way to honour the departed, however in times gone by this would also include watching to see if the dead would rise again. Even to this day, the deceased is laid out in their finest clothes, traditionally in the parlour of their home and loved ones gather for prayers and respects, keeping the dead company until they are buried.

Household Rituals

Every household would have its own rituals and traditions on the passing of a loved one and many still do. Most common however, was the opening of the bedroom window to allow the spirit of the departed to escape the confines of their body and home and pass on to the next realm. No one was to stand between the dead and the window as this would block the path to eternal rest and anyone who did so would be cursed forever more. Mirrors would be covered or turned to the wall, so the soul would not become trapped within. Clocks would be stopped at the time of death to prevent bad luck and as a mark of respect, because if a clock in the house was to stop of its own accord, another imminent death in the family would occur. .

Burial

As the departed left for their final journey, where and how they were buried was not as straightforward as it seems. In the Stone Age, the position you were buried in depended entirely on your status. You could be lying down, sitting, or if a great warrior, standing up for eternity. In the Bronze Age, beliefs changed and fire was deemed the only way to destroy the body and release the soul to the spirit realm. In the Middle Ages, if it was thought that you would return from the dead and devour the living, you would be buried in un-consecrated ground, bones broken and weighed down. Up until very recently, Infants who passed on without baptism or those who took their own lives would not be entitled to the rituals of waking, blessing and consecrated burial and would be buried, often in the still of night outside of the cemetery walls or in unmarked graves.

So, we closed our west facing windows and turned mirrors, so souls were not trapped. We paid Sin Eaters to take our transgressions and clear a path to Heaven. We left food as offerings to the *Sidhe* and the departed that they may look favorably upon us. We hired Keeners to cry at wakes so as not to invoke the Hounds of Hell, sent to collect the dead and take them to eternal torment. All in the name of saving our souls.

The fate of the spirit is of more concern to the Irish than death itself and over the centuries protection of the soul has taken precedence over anything else. Sometimes it doesn't matter what protections are put in place however, as the malevolent search for souls by the likes of the Dullahan and the Sluagh is too powerful and relentless. All we can do is the best we can in this life, maybe close the odd window at the right time, oh, and carry a bit of gold in our pockets – just in case!

Piseógs – The Curse of the Irish

Every culture has its own form of folk magic, both dark and light. Whatever form the magic takes, the goal is the same, normally wishing to cause harm to another. In Ireland, these magicks are known as *Piseógs* (*Pish-ogues*). The name is commonly used to cover all superstitions, but in reality, a *Piseóg* has much darker connotations. It is an Irish curse (although sometimes used for protection) designed for maximum impact, cast by a foe, a neighbour with a grudge or even the fairies themselves.

Much folk magic uses an external force, such as summoning a demon to do one's bidding, or in Jewish folklore, writing an intention on a piece of paper and placing it in the mouth of a Golem who will then carry out the required action.

Piseógs are different. It is thought that the very intention of wanting to cause harm is enough to actually make that wish would come to pass. Although often a catalyst (much like the Voodoo Doll) is used, it is not believed to have power itself. It is meant to be seen by the intended victim, to strike fear into the core of their very soul. This is where the power lies – in causing terror.

Many *Piseógs* reflect the nature of Irish Agricultural life. Curses are placed on farmers, crops and cattle and the catalyst is quite often an egg. Are they true curses, or simply a trick of the mind caused by fear and panic?

Your cows aren't giving any milk. Is it because a jealous competitor has put a *Piseóg* on you and used a cursed three-legged milking stool in his shed to drain your herd dry?

Your cattle are breeding stillborn and diseased calves. Is it because a neighbour has rubbed a cursed egg on their own stillborn calf, pierced the egg and left it your hay for your cattle to feed from?

Are you having no luck in your new house because an egg was cursed and left on your path by the fairies who did not want you to build there? Did the breaking of this egg release bad energy?

A farmer sees eggs laying in the hay he feeds to his cattle, or left lying in his ploughed potato fields. Immediately he believes he has been cursed, a neighbour has doomed him to fail. So, what can he do but try and remove the terror. The farmer destroys the hay or the drills he had ready for planting. As a result, the cattle are not fed and die or the crops aren't sown. The farm is destroyed by the hand of the farmer himself. The curse is a success.

Whether it is whole, or part animal carcasses being hung from your gate to curse the land, the mutterings of the malicious cursing you to never have a day's luck, or a *Piseóg* placed on your home for ill health or poverty, one thing is for sure. In Irish folk magic words are powerful and the tool to facilitate the message more powerful still. Nothing however, is more potent than the fear and horror they create in the minds of the victims.

The mental anguish of the terrified recipient and the destruction they cause as a result is far more effective than any direct attack could ever be. Whether the curse itself is real, or whether psychological impact is the key, *Piseógs* work. Keep that in mind if you hear the crack of an eggshell under your foot and stop and ask yourself, who did you upset?

The Hungry Grass

If you have ever found yourself in an Irish country pub and listened in on a conversation or two, you may have heard mention of *Feár Gortach* (*Fair Gor-toc*) or The Hungry Grass. If you are foolish enough to step on the Hungry Grass, you will be doomed to suffer insatiable hunger until you die.

In the late 1840s, the Irish Famine took hold and man, woman and child were left to starve to death as a direct result of the Potato Blight and a misuse of resources under British rule. Over a million people died in poverty, starvation and agony. These victims of famine were thrown into mass graves, usually fields, their souls forever to be in torment.

All over Ireland, there were hundreds of mass graves, or Famine Graveyards as they became known. All were originally un-consecrated, although in later years many became memorialised and recognised consecrated ground. Some however, remained buried in cold, unhallowed ground, souls crying out for their purgatory to end. Over the top of these burial sites, the grass grew, and it was cursed. It was hungry.

Anyone spending time in Ireland will be told at some point of a short cut and inevitably, this will lead to crossing a field. From Cork to Kilkenny and Galway to Connemara, you will hear tales of people losing their way on such short cuts and being caught by the Hungry Grass. A young man walking home, a sunny day, strolling through the field, found days later, not knowing where he is, starving and confused. He is taken home and no amount of nursing or food can save him. Others are so overwhelmed by the touch of the cursed grass that they drop dead of hunger where they stand. The victims of the Famine have become predatory, seeking to drag others into their hell and your only protection is to carry a crust of bread in your pocket - and even this may not be enough to save you.

Next time you are walking through a field, ask yourself is that a brush of grass around your ankles, or the bony fingers of the ravenous seeking company as misery requires......

A million unheard voices
Starved and damned to hell
If you set foot on the Hungry Grass
They'll take you there as well.

A million unheard voices
Cry the agony of their final hour
If you set foot on The Hungry Grass
Your soul they will devour.

HEROES AND VILLIANS, SAINTS AND SINNERS

Saint Patrick – Man, Myth, Saint and Legend

On 17 March every year, the whole world finds a little Irish inside of them and celebrates the anniversary of the death of Ireland's Patron Saint, Patrick. This day has become a global commercial phenomenon, with even the most revered of world historical monuments lit up in green to celebrate a man whose life remains an enigma to many, the man and legend heavily intertwined.

Saint Patrick was born Maewyn Succat in the latter 4th Century in what was then known as Briton. From a high-ranking Roman family, his father Calphurnius was a Deacon and his mother Conchessa had strong links with the Church.

It was odd therefore, that the young Maewyn was not active in the Church and was not raised under religious doctrine. Also unusual for a family of such high standing, the boy received very little education -something he would reflect on with regret in later life.

Life was very much uneventful, that is until he turned sixteen. Taken prisoner by Irish Pirates, Saint Patrick was sold into slavery in Ireland. He was sent to work in the North of Ireland as a Shepherd for a Chieftain known as Milchu. Saint Patrick's Master was a Druid Priest, and in his years of captivity, Saint Patrick became well versed in Pagan worship, and practices, as well becoming as fluent in the native Irish tongue.

Witness to Pagan rituals and left with much time alone on the hills of Antrim, Saint Patrick turned to God in his hour of need and prayed long and hard. After six years, Saint Patrick received a vision, some say an angel, telling him to escape. Stowing away on a ship, Patrick found himself reunited with his family.

The ordeal of kidnap and slavery had changed the young man. After all, he had seen and heard Patrick was determined to rid Ireland of Paganism and bring Christianity to the shores of the Emerald Isle. With focus and direction, he set off for Auxerre in France to enter the priesthood and study under the guidance of Saint Germain. For many years, Saint Patrick studied and prayed, never forgetting his ultimate purpose.

In 431 A.D, under the recommendation of Saint Germain, Pope St. Celestine I renamed Maewyn Patritius or Patrick in expectancy of him fulfilling his role as the Father of the Irish people- a role given after Pallidius had failed in fear to convert the Tribes of Ireland to Christianity and had abandoned his sacred duty.

Following preparations and further study, Patrick set sail for Ireland and for a renewed battle with the Druid Chieftains and their unrelenting warriors. Choosing to begin his work in the place of his enslavement, Patrick's way was fraught with hostility and danger.

It was during this period of opposition that Saint Patrick came into his own. Speaking to the Irish in their own tongue, Patrick declared that their faith kept them enslaved under the power of the Druid Chieftains and that believing in God and living a Christian life would set them free.

Called to Tara to meet with the Great Chieftains, along the way Saint Patrick's Crusade gathered strength in numbers, heightened by the apparent miracles he was performing and through his own charismatic speeches and humble manner.

The Oracles of the Druids had spoken of the messenger of Christ coming to Erin and they were more than prepared for Patrick's arrival. They had demanded that all fires be extinguished until a new flame announcing Druid victory was lit in the Royal House. The meeting was at Easter, and Patrick set up camp on Slane Hill opposite Tara where he lit the Paschal fire as part of the Easter vigil.

Outraged the Druid Priests cried out that if their own gods did not quench the Holy flame that night they would be doomed for it to burn on Ireland's shores forever. Many attempts were made by the Pagans to douse the fire, but it was all to no avail and Patrick remained unscathed despite the continued assaults on his camp.

Saint Patrick began his procession to Tara, with the Druids and their Magicians using all their power to block his path. So dark was the magic, the sky became covered with black clouds of apocalyptic proportions. Undeterred, the Bishop of Ireland prayed until rays of sunlight broke through and dispersed the clouds.

In a final attempt to retain control, the Arch-Druid Lochru, used his dark magic to rise high into the air. Saint Patrick prayed until the Priest was dashed on the rocks below. Knowing that a great power was in their presence and that their prophecy had come to pass, the High Kings gave their permission for Christianity to be preached to the people of Ireland. It was during his time at Tara that Patrick picked a Shamrock from the ground to use as a symbol of the Holy Trinity.

Saint Patrick began to travel the length and breadth of Ireland, facing resentment, imprisonment and violence every step of the way. Patrick's reputation and news of his miracles began to spread quickly however, as more and more of the Irish turned their back on Paganism and were instilled with Christian hope and faith.

Having spent much time in Munster, baptising, teaching and founding Churches and schools, Patrick continued on, journeying to the hill now known as Croagh Patrick, a place of Holiness and Pilgrimage. Here he began a retreat of 40 days and nights of abstinence and prayer, all the while resisting temptation from the demons and darkness around him.

Having rid Ireland of Paganism, and having brought hope and peace to the Irish, freeing them of slavery, Saint Patrick was called to his eternal reward at the end of the fifth Century, on the 17th of March.

What of the snakes you ask? There are many stories and legends, whether true or parables to explain his work who can say? In his own writings "Confessio" and the "Epistola ad Coroticum" no mention is made of this particular miracle.

Most likely, the snakes are an analogy for the Paganism that Saint Patrick drove from Ireland's shores, what is fact and what is legend we will never know for sure. What we do know is that for over 1500 years, a Roman-Briton slave who returned to Irish lands to bring Christianity to the people has become a beacon for celebration, not just in Ireland, but throughout the world.

So on 17 March, raise your glass and remember the man, the myth and the legend, whatever your beliefs and enjoy being Irish, even if it is just for one day!

Sláinte!

Brian Boru – Ireland's Thousand Year Hero

A thousand years ago, on the 23rd of March 1014, Ireland's last great High King was slain at the Battle of Clontarf. Bards, writers, painters and sculptors have all been enthralled and inspired by the legendary and heroic tales of Brian Boru. Like so much of Irish legend and folklore, the stories have real foundation and hold a place of great importance in Irish History.

Brian Boru was born Brian Cennétig to Lorcáin, King of Thomond and Leader of the *Dál gCais* Clan, known as the Dalcassians in Killaloe, County Clare. He was the youngest of twelve sons, and when his father died at the hands of the Vikings, older brother Mathgamain took the throne.

The Vikings were very much focused on success in Munster and particularly Limerick due to the significance of its port and access along the River Shannon. After they had imposed severe taxes, with Brian's assistance, Mathgamain fought back and seized the Rock of Cashel from the Norsemen, leading to him being crowned King of Munster, taking the title from the *Uí Néill* clan who had reigned for six hundred years.

During conflicts between both the Norse 'Ostermen' and rival chieftains, Mathgamain was slain. In retaliation, Brian assassinated the King of the Ostermen in Limerick and became King of Munster. A skilled and persuasive leader, Brian held Munster alone, unchallenged, and had his first victory as King in battle over the Vikings at the Battle of Sulcoit in Tipperary.

King Brian marched onto Connaught and Leinster and entered into conflict with the High King Mael Sechnaill mac Domnaill. When Brian took control of Leinster, Mael Sechnaill ceded to Brian's authority for reasons that were never recorded, and the King of Leinster was overthrown. King Brian was named *Ard Ri*, the High King of Ireland in the year 1002.

Years of battle and politics followed, both with rival Chieftains and the Vikings, however in order to keep his followers loyal, King Brian used tactics unfamiliar with his predecessors. Instead of taxes and enforced removal of valuables to fund his wars, Brian asked for tributes, which he then ploughed into the restoration of monasteries, schools and libraries that had been destroyed by the Norsemen throughout Ireland.

The High King of Ireland then became known as Brian, King of Tributes, or Brian Boru. A spiritual man and a man of words and music on the one hand and a formidable warrior on the other, King Brian was always at threat from both the domestic and foreign enemy.

The High King of Ireland held an uneasy acknowledgement from the Chieftains for only a short time and the Vikings were not surrendering. Indeed, the Vikings had begun converting to Christianity and were forming alliances through inter-marriage and political integration. One such Chieftain, Máel Mórda mac Murchada had resented Brian and began a rebellion in 1012. Máel then formed an alliance with Ulster and began an attack on Meath. Although King Brian tried to assist the High King Máel Sechnaill in his defence, he was forced to retreat back to Munster.

In 1014, the Irish Chieftain rivals of Leinster and Dublin and the Norsemen gathered and created an alliance against Brian Boru, fully convinced that the great High King of Ireland would return. Brian himself had a mixed army of his loyal followers, Irish men, Munster Vikings who had integrated into the Irish clans and Viking mercenaries. Most surprising were the men of the Province of Meath, commanded by his old rival Mael Sechnaill mac Domnaill.

Confident he would succeed, Brian Boru sent an advance attack party to south Leinster, however a disagreement had led to the withdrawal of Mael Sechnaill mac Domnaill and his troops, which in turn steered directly to the Battle of Clontarf.

Two sides evenly matched in strength and numbers, the battle began on Palm Sunday, on 18 April. Thus begins the blurring of legend and history. The battle itself was arduous and there were heavy losses on both sides, however stories of magic and a titanic battle of good versus evil have grown to legendary proportion.

It was said that the Viking arrows were anointed with the blood of dragons, that witches, and demons waited impatiently to claim the fallen in battle. It was also written that the banshee of the House of Munster would appear to forewarn of the death of warriors aligned to Brian Boru. Whether supernatural or man-made circumstance, this was to be Brian Boru's final battle.

King Brian was advancing in years by this stage and no longer able to take his place on the battlefield, choosing instead to pray for the spiritual well-being and victory of his troops in his tent. In an unfortunate twist of events, the Vikings facing defeat were fleeing and a Norse Commander known as Brodir happened upon the King's tent. Brodir entered the camp and murdered King Brian Boru, High King of Ireland as he knelt in prayer on Good Friday, the 23rd of April 1014.

Brian Boru's remains were taken to Swords in Dublin and then escorted to Armagh where he is believed to be buried in Saint

Patrick's Cathedral. Although King Brian was slain, the Battle of Clontarf was a victory and Ireland remained under Irish rule.

After this the title of High King became honorary and the Vikings that remained integrated into Christianity and the Irish ways. Brian Boru however would not be forgotten. Stories, poems and artwork have carried through the centuries, each depicting the hero, the warrior, the legend and the man. Official annals and other documents exist in Ireland and Denmark and his name can be seen throughout Munster and Ireland.

So this day we remember the thousand year hero of Ireland, Brian Boru. He is, and always will be, the most successful High King of Munster and the Last Great High King of Ireland.

The Wizard Earl of Kildare

When you think of wizards, Harry Potter and Merlin may be the first names that spring to mind, however Ireland has not been without its own Sorcerers. When you think of Irish legend, sometimes the line between fact and folklore is a shimmering tale of enchantment, as is the case with The Wizard Earl of Kildare.

The Earl Gerald Fitzgerald was born in the early part of the 16th Century and sent to be educated in Europe where he embraced the Renaissance. During this time, his preferred studies were in Medicine, Astronomy and Metallurgy and after some time Gerald discovered he had a penchant for Alchemy.

After a number of years travelling through Europe and after the death of Henry VIII, lost lands in Ireland were returned to the Fitzgerald family and *Gerod Earla*, as the Irish knew him, took up residence at Kilkea Castle in County Kildare.

Gerald spent years quietly studying and practising the Occult until his wife became overcome with curiosity and demanded to be a witness to his feats of Dark Magic. The Wizard Earl agreed, with the warning that if she were to show fear, then his wife would never see him again. He then set about three tests to see if her resolve was strong enough to outweigh her fear.

For the first test, Gerald commanded the River Greese to swell up and flood the Banqueting hall in which they sat. The waters rose to the mouth of his wife and she did not flinch.

Satisfied, he moved on to the second test in which he summoned the form of a long-departed friend. The dead man strode through the hall, stopped in front of the Countess Fitzgerald and took her hand. He then walked out through the wall at the other end.

When she showed no reaction, the Earl moved on to the third test in which he conjured a serpent like monster that wrapped itself around his stoic wife. Once again, there was no fear and so Gerald Fitzgerald made the decision to show her how he could transform his very being.

Gerald told his wife to close her eyes, and when she heard him stamp three times, to open them. She did so and a black bird appeared before her. The bird flew up to her shoulder and began to sing. It was at this point the castle cat pounced and the Countess fainted with shock. When she was revived, there was no sign of either the cat or the bird.

Legend says that *Gerod Earla* was never seen again, yet some historians believe the Earl lived out the remainder of his life in semi-captivity in London only returning back to Ireland for burial in 1585.

The story did not end there, as it is believed the Wizard Earl and his closest men at arms have laid in an enchanted sleep in a cave for centuries under the Rath on the hill of Mullaghmast, just north of Kilkea Castle.

Every seven years the Earl Gerald Fitzgerald rises up and mounts his white horse, shod in silver. He rides across the Curragh with his men, bringing fear to the travellers and farmers in their wake, with sightings have appeared as late as the end of the nineteenth century.

It is said that one brave soul entered the Cave and began to draw his sword from its sheath for protection. This act awoke the Earl from his slumber and he asked, "Is it time yet?" The trespasser sheathed his sword and replied it was not and Gerald returned to sleep.

"Time for what?" you might ask. The legend says that when the silver shoes of the white steed are worn to nothing, the enchantment will break, and Gerald Fitzgerald will rise up in full strength to rid Ireland of its enemies.

Fact, folklore or all of the above, the legend has stood the test of time and Kilkea Castle remains. If you should be visiting in the seventh year and see Gerald thundering past on his white horse, take a look at its silver shoes. If they are no more, pack your bag and run, as the Wizard Earl will be coming home.

ON TRIAL FOR WITCHCRAFT – IRISH WOMEN OF POWER OR SORCERY?

Were some of Ireland's most powerful and notorious women in fact witches? Or were they victims of their own success falling foul of the jealous and fearful?

Alice Kyteler

Long before the publication of *Malleus Maleficarum*, attention was brought to bear on the small medieval town of Kilkenny in the Kingdom of Ossory. One of the earliest ever recorded witch trials took place in the early 14th century against a local businesswoman and serial bride by the name of Alice Kyteler - and what a sensational trial it was. So who was the local entrepreneur and femme fatale who caused uproar in the Irish legal system and brought the Ecclesiastical authorities of Ireland to their knees?

Alice Kyteler's family were Flemish brokers and they had settled in Kilkenny sometime towards the end of the 13th century with just one child, a daughter. Alice learned the ropes of the family business and grew up to be very shrewd, so it came as no surprise that her first husband was an affluent local businessman and financier by the name of William Outlaw.

Believed to have married in 1280 when Alice would have been only sixteen or so, they went on to have a son, also called William. The banker's wife groomed her son for great things and by an early age, he had gained positions of authority within the local community. By 1302, William's father was dead and Alice was already onto her second marriage. Husband number two was another moneylender by the name of Adam le Blund, from the market town of Callan on the Kilkenny/Tipperary county borders.

Both parties were already wealthy before the union; however, marriage brought them a new level of power and prosperity. The couple's wealth and status had left feelings of acrimony running high in the parish and rumours had already began to circulate that Alice's first husband had not died from natural causes. The locals were convinced that Alice and Adam had in fact, committed murder.

The fire of fear and distrust aimed at Alice Kyteler was beginning to take hold; however, it would appear that Alice and the events surrounding her were adding fuel to the growing flames. In 1307, Adam le Blund relinquished all legal entitlement to his own wealth and gave what was effectively full Power of Attorney to his stepson William, together with the complete nullification of William's debts agreements. This incident was deemed all the more suspicious as Adam had offspring of his own from a prior marriage and was in seemingly good mental and physical health. Two years later, he was dead.

The year 1309 saw Alice wed for the third time. Richard de Valle was an affluent landowner from the neighbouring county of Tipperary and once again, the marital union was short lived. A seemingly fit and well Richard died mysteriously, leaving all his wealth to Alice. The son of the unfortunate deceased, also called Richard, kept hold of the assets and was the subject of legal proceedings, as the widow demanded her rightful wealth.

By the time Alice Kyteler married yet another wealthy landlord, Sir John le Poer, the local rumour mill was in overdrive and the whispering of foul play continued. In frighteningly similar circumstances to her first three husbands, John's health began to decline, in spite of his relatively young age. John's fingernails and toenails were discolouring and falling out, he was rapidly going bald, and the little hair he had left was devoid of pigmentation. As his ailments increased and his already poor health took a decided turn for the worse, two game changing events took place. First of all, with no regard for his own blood kin, John made a will bequeathing all his money and assets to Alice and her son William. The second, fearing for his life, John turned to the church for help. By 1324, he was dead and the whispers had turned to shouts of witchcraft

Despite marrying prosperous landowners, Alice insisted that she remain in her birthplace on St. Kieran's Street in Kilkenny. As a rich wife and ultimately an incredibly wealthy serial widow, Alice did not need to work, however her focus was on building and maintaining a thriving business. She continued with her practice of moneylending, made easier by having the perfect location to conduct her affairs. Kyteler's Inn wasn't just any old hostelry, it was a meeting place for local businessmen, who all vied for the attention of the bewitching Alice, showering her with gifts and money. It should therefore come as no surprise that this was the very place Alice set eyes on her ill-fated husbands to be.

Whilst the attention of so many of the wealthy local male population was scintillating for Alice, she was a canny businesswoman first and foremost. She hired the most luscious and alluring young women to work in her premises, enticing men from their wives and responsibilities to spend their money in Kyteler's Inn, making her establishment the most successful in Kilkenny. It was also here in the Inn that Alice was said to work her sorcery and that her patrons were bewitched by Alice and her alleged coven.

Contrary to popular belief, the Church often turned a blind eye to sorcery, accepting that some forms of *Malficium* were minor offences and that the medical benefits offered by those who practiced such arts outweighed the 'crime'. As such, the local authorities and not the Church, except in the case of direct heretical doctrine, dealt with any issues relating to witchcraft.

Unfortunately for Alice, this all changed when Pope John XXII came to the Papal Throne in 1316. He was genuinely terrified of witchcraft and was convinced his life was in jeopardy, leading to the granting of sweeping powers to his Inquisitors. Pope John XXII published a definitive list of practices that would constitute heresy and subsequent prosecution by the Church, particularly in relation to demon worship and pacts with the devil. Unfortunately for Alice, this canon law reached Ireland and in particular, Richard Ledrede, the Bishop of Ossory.

Whether out of bitterness of being cheated from their respective inheritance or genuine concern that Alice Kyteler was indeed a witch, the children of her last three deceased husbands joined together and called upon the assistance of Richard Ledrede.

Richard was a devout Christian and fanatical with seeking out and punishing heretics. He was unhappy that respect for the Church and canon law were fading and that the law of the land took precedent. He had the necessary background to implement Church doctrine and proceed with charges of heresy against Alice and her son William Outlaw, however he was up against resistance from local law enforcement and Alice's very powerful contacts.

Having heard the allegations from Alice's stepchildren, Ledrede went ahead and charged Alice, her maid Petronella and her son William with heresy. The charges included denying the Faith, desecration of the Church with black magic rituals, sorcery, demonic animal sacrifice, murder, controlling members of the local community with potions and spells and fornicating with a demon known by many names including Robin Artisson, in exchange for power and prosperity.

Richard's first attempt at arrest was thwarted by the Chancellor of Ireland, Roger Outlaw, a relative of Alice's first husband. He advised Ledrede that there could be no warrant issued for the arrests without the accused having first been excommunicated for at least 40 days and a public hearing. Meanwhile the well-timed intervention of another relation by marriage, Sir Arnold de Poer, senior steward of Kilkenny allowed Alice to flee to Dublin and saw the imprisonment of Richard Ledrede.

While Richard was in prison, the whole of the diocese of Ossory saw an embargo on funerals, baptisms and marriage. As the majority of the population believed in Hell and eternal damnation, the public outcry was too much and the Bishop of Ossory was released. Incarceration left Ledrede incensed and he heightened his efforts to prosecute Alice, her son and maid by involving the Justice of Ireland, who insisted upon a full witch trial.

William Outlaw pleaded guilty to the charges of heresy, illegal money lending, adultery and perverting the course of justice. His punishment was to attend three masses a day, donate to the poor and agree to reroof the cathedral with lead.

In the meantime, Alice had absconded, and the trial continued in her absence. The alleged depths of her depravity and heresy began to be revealed to the court. The witch Kyteler was said to have used a human skull to brew her potions, with ingredients including parts of corpses, the innards of fowl, worms and insects and the clothing of deceased infants. The concoctions were said to rouse her innocent victims to do her bidding, with acts of love, hatred or murder.

Alice and her coven were said to have conducted black masses in the churches, sacrificed and dissected livestock to bargain with demons at crossroads and Alice herself was accused of continued carnal relations with a powerful demon in order to maintain her position of influence over the local community.

The final accusations were of the murder of each of her four husbands. Evidence regarding her last husband, John le Poer was put forward. He had no nails, they were ripped from their beds and left bleeding, all bodily hair had fallen out and he was completed withered away to a skeleton at the time of his death.

While Alice had disappeared, some say to England with the help of her well-positioned male acquaintances, her maid was not so fortunate. Petronella de Meath was tortured repeatedly in Kilkenny Jail until she confessed to being a witch and a member of the coven of Alice Kyteler. On the 3rd of November 1324, Petronella was the first woman in Ireland to be burned at the stake as a witch.

So, what of Alice? Well Alice Kyteler was never heard of again – whether she used witchcraft to cloak her whereabouts or was helped abroad by calling on infatuated men of position we will never know.

What we do know, is that the accusations and the trial were very real indeed. They remain documented as they have been for centuries and the trial changed the balance of law and power back in favour of the Church.

The most exciting revelation of this account is that the locations remain. The Jail still stands, bars on windows. As you stand on the street, peering into the eerie darkness of the cold, cramped cells, a shiver runs up your spine at the realization there could be something ethereal staring back at you, perhaps the tormented blackened soul of Petronella de Meath. Kyteler's Inn is still the most famous hostelry in Kilkenny and the spirit of Alice is said to remain, watching over her establishment and the revelers within for eternity.

Was Alice Kyteler indeed a witch, or just the most successful and richest businesswoman in medieval Ireland? Perhaps if you come across her in Kyteler's Inn, you can ask her yourself!

Florence Newton, the Witch of Youghal

Another sensational witch trial for Ireland was that of Florence Newton in 1661. She was accused of enchanting Mary Langdon, the maid of a prominent figure in the town called John Pyne.

Florence had called to the house during the winter of 1660 asking for meat from the master's table. The maid refused, and the slighted beggar left muttering curses. When Florence met Mary Langdon on the street, she grabbed her and gave her a vicious kiss, after which time Mary became violently ill. She suffered seizures, visions and the house of her master became subject to poltergeist activity.

When Newton was brought into Mary's presence her sickness became worse and she began vomiting needles and nails. Mary claimed that Florence would appear in visions, sticking pins into her body. Newton was also accused of causing the death of her jailer through sorcery, as his widow accused Florence of kissing her husband on the hand shortly before he dropped dead.

So important was the trial of the Witch of Youghal that the Irish Attorney General came to Cork to preside and it was assumed that Florence was found guilty and hanged. You see, despite well-kept records of the beginning of the trial, the remainder of them vanished completely so we will never know exactly what happened to Florence Newton. Did she also use Sorcery to survive?

Biddy Early and the Magic Blue Bottle

Biddy Early was born in 1778 in Kilenena, County Clare and took her mother's maiden name. Ellen Early taught her daughter herbal cures, however both parents died when Biddy was sixteen and she was left in poverty and living in the poorhouse.

Marginalised for being aloof, rumour had it that Biddy had been talking to the fairies since she was a child and could control them at will. A good-looking woman, Biddy met the first of her four husbands at market, a man twice her age.

Already making a name for herself as a healer, Biddy also opened a successful Shebeen, were the local folk would drink illicit alcohol and play cards. Within five years, her husband Pat had died from alcohol consumption and she married her stepson John who also died from alcohol related issues. Her third husband died in 1868 when she was 70 and in 1869, she married a man in his thirties in exchange for a cure.

Biddy's healing powers seemed to have centred on a mysterious blue bottle that was supposedly brought to her by a dead relative from the fairies. No one could touch the bottle and only true believers would receive help from Biddy.

If she knew you had been to a physician, you were thrown out and priests in disguise would be regularly hunted away as they tried to get to the root of her power. Biddy publicly denounced the Catholic Church and was accused and charged with Witchcraft in 1865, which was very unusual this late on.

Fear took hold of those who had agreed to testify, and Biddy was acquitted. On her deathbed she repented and at her funeral a gathering of priests asked the community to pray for the soul of Biddy Early.

Her cottage stands in ruins and her grave in Feakle is unmarked, however her blue bottle was not to be seen after she died. Did the fairies reclaim the source of Biddy Early's power?

Petticoat Loose

Mary Hannigan was born the only child of a well to do family in the early part of the 19th Century. She was an extremely tall and stout woman who was well able to handle manual farm work. Mary also loved to dance, however with her stature no man could handle her except for one, whom she ended up marrying.

Mary earned her nickname of Petticoat Loose after one raucous session of drinking and dancing after a wedding. Spinning around in a drunken whirl the buttons of her skirt snagged and the whole thing came apart, falling to the floor. Mary was laughed at and jeered until she punched and kicked at those who dare laugh at her misfortune.

Petticoat Loose and her husband had a troubled time running their farm and rumours were rife that she was a witch. Stories of their milk turning blue when added to tea were rampant and they lost business.

About a year after her marriage, Mary and a servant girl were milking the herd when a scream was heard from one of the fields. The milkmaid ran towards the sound; however, a milking stool hitting her firmly in the back stopped her.

Mary loomed over her and told the frightened girl to mind her own business. Strangely, after that night her husband was never seen again. It was generally believed that the evil woman and her lover had planned the murder and he had seen it through.

Months later Mary was in a drinking match in the local tavern with some labourers who she drank clean under the table. She cheered and gloated her success – then dropped dead on the spot. There was a huge village wake for Mary, but no priest was ever summoned.

Several years later at another village gathering, a man stepped out for some air and froze as he saw Petticoat Loose stood watching him. The locals were terrified and refused to leave until daylight. She was regularly seen on the road and would flag down horse and carts. One man refused, and she jumped aboard regardless. She rose up and bellowed that she was carrying a ton weight in both hands and on her legs. The cart ground to a halt and the horse died of exhaustion due to the bewitching. Petticoat Loose ran away cackling.

People were so scared they travelled with religious protections and hazel twigs but finally they called in a priest to be rid of Petticoat Loose once and for all. He demanded she speak her name where upon he doused her with Holy Water and banished her to Bay Lough in the Knockmealdown Mountains where she was sentenced to empty the lake with a thimble.

Some say she remains there, serving her penance, others will not venture in for fear of her pulling them under as she laughs. Many say she transforms into a half horse, half- human to roam and terrorize the night. One thing is for sure, no one can ever say Petticoat Loose is gone for good

Skilled, manipulative and powerful all, but were they Witches? That knowledge is lost forever, by way of Witchcraft or otherwise!

The Pirate Queen of Ireland

Being Ireland is most feared and successful pirate was not a job for the faint hearted – or a man. In the 16th century lived a red headed Celtic warrior and pirate, leading men into battle time and time again, amassing property and riches, married twice with lovers on the side, rebelling against the English crown. A formidable enemy of intimidation and brute force, controlling the coastlines of Ireland and

Scotland, murdering all around and oh yes, a woman. You heard me. Let me tell you about Grace O'Malley, the Sea Queen of Connaught.

Grace O'Malley was born into a thriving shipping and trading family in 1530, well that was the official name, but it had another – piracy.

The young Grace's determination to be a part of her father's successful enterprise was discouraged, so in an act of defiance she cut off her long red hair and was known as Grace the bald or *Granuaile*. On one return journey from Spain that Grace had undertaken with her father, they were boarded by enemy pirates and Grace was ordered to hide. Of course, she disobeyed and climbed the rigging instead. On seeing her father being attacked, Grace jumped screaming from the rigging onto the assailant's back and so began her life as the formidable Sea Queen.

Married at 16 to Donal O'Flaherty as a suitable match due to his wealth and ambition, Grace had three children by him and their stronghold was known as 'The Cock's Castle' in Lough Lorrib. The Joyce clan were determined to take the fort and attacked, killing Donal in the process. What they hadn't bargained for was a violent, angry widow who wasn't giving up her home to anyone.

The furious Grace personally commanded her husband's men and supervised the stripping of lead from the roof, melted it down and made shot to fire at her attackers below. The Joyce clan were so impressed, that they withdrew and renamed the place 'The Hen's Castle', a name still in use today. Her success was short-lived however, as her two sons took the property and wealth from her.

A tougher and wiser woman, Grace took a couple of hundred men and ran her piracy operations from Clare Island. Still not ready for complete independence, Grace sought out a further suitable marriage to increase her assets and standing. She wed Risdeárd an Iarainn Bourke, also known as Iron Richard and lived with him at Rockfleet Castle, a strategically valuable stronghold in County Mayo. The new Mrs. Bourke was no fool however, and their marriage was a one-year contract under Brehon Law. When the year was up, she tossed Richard out on his ear and in the divorce, Grace took possession of the castle.

This was not a woman to be messed with and she even gave birth to Richard's son Tibbot on the high seas. In less than a day her ship was attacked by Turkish pirates and after casting the gibbering captain of her vessel aside, brandished a musket and blew every Turk in her sight away. The enemy ship was seized, and the remaining crew killed.

Grace was quite the promiscuous woman and one of her lovers was a shipwrecked casualty of one her attacks, a much younger man called Hugh de Lacy. He was murdered by the McMahon clan of Ballycroy during a hunting expedition, an act they would soon regret.

Driven into a frenzied rage over the murder of her lover, Grace personally tracked the killers to the Holy Island of Caher in Mayo. There, everyone who had crossed her died at the grieving woman's hand and all the boats were burned. This was not enough revenge for the fearless Grace however, so she travelled to Ballycroy and stormed Doona Castle, the family home of the McMahons and took it for herself.

All the while Grace was maintaining her hold over the shores and seas, demanding taxes from fishermen, raiding islands as far as Scotland and operating a protection racket which saw ships being boarded and cash or cargo being handed over in exchange for safe passage. Those who did not comply were savagely beaten or murdered by order of the Pirate Queen.

Not satisfied that her henchmen were instilling enough terror on the waters, Grace hired a brutal and vicious gang of mercenaries known as the Gallowglass Warriors. These men were animals, bludgeoning and slashing everything and everyone who got in their way with their weapon of choice, the double headed Sparthe Axe, leaving a trail of blood-soaked carnage in their wake.

In the late 16th century, the Spanish were at war with the English off the Irish coast and Grace was not going to be collateral damage, so she took her men and butchered hundreds of Spanish soldiers on board ships near to her home at Clare Island.

As Grace O'Malley became more powerful and formidable, she upped the ante and began attacking castles and strongholds along the shores of Ireland, to the point where the English crown could no longer turn a blind eye to her criminal activities - particularly when most of the male clan chiefs had already surrendered land and wealth to Queen Elizabeth I.

The Governor of Connaught, Sir Richard Bingham was particularly angered at the Sea Queen of his province and her exploits. He sent men to attack her fortress, where upon she supervised the pouring of hot oil onto her would be captors and they withdrew. They didn't get too far however, as Grace lit a beacon signalling her ships at sea to destroy the retreating English. Not bad for a female pirate who was now almost sixty years of age!

Outraged, Bingham arranged for the capture of Grace's son and brother, with a view to holding them to ransom so that she would have to surrender her lands and spoils. What he didn't bank on, was Grace setting sail for England and an audience with Queen Elizabeth.

The meeting between the two strong willed and fiery redheads took place on 6 September 1593, carried out in Latin as neither woman spoke the other's native tongue. Without any bloodshed and just using her sharp mind and political skills, Grace O'Malley persuaded Queen Elizabeth to not only order Bingham to release her family and restore property, but also to grant permission for her to continue with her rebellious activities.

Grace continued to run her operation, switching sides as suited her needs to increase her holdings and wealth. Finally, after over half a century of violent, bloody piracy and conquest, Granuaile retired to Rockfleet Castle, never defeated, rich beyond measure and with a string of lovers at her disposal. She died in around 1603, in her seventies, notorious and still feared.

Immortalised in poems, plays, books and songs, when it comes to legendary kickass Pirate Queens, there is only one and her name is Grace O'Malley.

Murder on the Path to Sainthood

Saint Kevin of Glendalough is known for the founding of the Wicklow Monastery and his love of animals; however his rise to Sainthood was not without incident.

Born in the final years of the fifth century, the young boy may have been deemed holy at birth, however his behaviour was anything but Christian. Kevin was a foul tempered, difficult child who hated people and preferred the company of animals.

Kevin was sent to the monastery at the age of just seven and upon being ordained pledged a life of abstinence and began to live in a small cave as a hermit until he was forced back into the community due to his miracles.

The young man was blessed with good looks and brought attention to himself and a local woman, Kathleen set her sights on seducing the poor monk. The harlot used to dress provocatively in red and follow the celibate Kevin until one day she followed him into the woods and pushed him too far.

Desperate not to fall to temptation, Kevin threw himself into a bed of nettles and in temper tore some off and beat Kathleen towards the edge of the lake, whereupon he forced her into the water and drowned her.

The tale of Kathleen's murder has been reported for centuries and both poets and musicians alike have immortalised the tale. Long after the death and canonization of Saint Kevin, the failed seductress Kathleen still haunts the ruins of Glendalough Monastery.

Murder at Ballyvolane House

In 1730, the elderly Andrew and Jane St Leger had rented the grand house in Cork from the owners. They kept their valuables in a treasure chest in their bedroom as was typical of the time.

Butler Timothy Croneen and maid Joan Condon became focused on the hoard and together they plotted the murder of the old couple. On 4 November 1730, Joan allegedly held a candle as Timothy shot Andrew St Leger and brutally stabbed his wife Jane multiple times with a sword.

In order to create an alibi, the two buried the chest they had stolen in the shrubbery of the house and returned to their quarters, so it appeared strangers had committed the heinous crime.

The alarm was raised, and shock spread through Cork. It was traditional that employees would ride on the carriage carrying their deceased master/mistress and so the murderers found themselves on the day of funeral riding with the bodies of their victims.

The family dog, a spaniel followed behind the hearse carriage, crying pitifully and unnerving Joan Condon in the process. Worried she would crack under the pressure, Timothy Croneen jumped down and picked up the dog. Once the procession was out of sight he slit the dog's throat and tossed it into a ditch.

Croneen caught up with the cortege, however with the spaniel's disappearance the other servants began to take an interest in the shifty butler and maid. A ford was reached, and the horses refused to cross the river, despite every effort. Mutterings began that only witches could not cross the river and was there someone on the carriage causing the horses' distress.

Finally, the horses crossed but suspicion against the two continued to mount and the staff became very vocal in their belief that the authorities should look no further than Ballyvolane for their killers.

Panicking Croneen and Condon fled the house without their loot and headed for Cork Harbour where they boarded a boat for France. A storm blew up and the vessel was unable to set sail and delayed departure for 24 hours.

Crazed with fear at this stage, the fugitives travelled up to Limerick Port, however as time passed their pictures had travelled the counties and they walked straight into an alert official who arrested them and returned them to Cork for trial. Both were tried and convicted of double murder and the theft of the treasure.

Timothy Croneen was hanged at Gallows Green, hung, drawn and quartered. His head was then placed on a spike as a warning to others at Cork. Joan Condon however was allegedly a different story. She was convicted of being a witch and was taken to a place within the shadow of the murder scene where she was burned at the stake. The treasure chest was never recovered. Were the servants right that they had a murderous witch in their midst?

The Dolocher

Going by the ominous name of Black Dog Prison, the gaol in the area now known as Cornmarket in Dublin was as notorious as it sounds. Opened at the very beginning of the eighteenth century, it became the main debtors' prison and immediately was a hive of corruption, mismanagement and abuse. Entirely run as a business enterprise, a prisoner could pay for the use of one of the flea-ridden beds, or else end up in the dank, rat-infested dungeons with only stale musty air to breathe.

One such inmate was a man known as Olocher. He was tried and convicted of the savage rape and murder of a woman and was incarcerated, awaiting his execution day. On the morning, he was due to be carried through the streets and hanged at Gallows Green in 1788, he was found dead in his cell.

There was outrage that Olocher had cheated his punishment and had found a way to commit suicide. Investigations took place, but no one could understand how the murdering fiend had gained the means to take his own life and avoid the gallows.

The following night a sentry was at his post near Cork Street when his cries tore through the night. He was found, falling into unconsciousness, in his own blood and looking to all intents and purposes as if he had been savagely attacked by a large vicious animal. When he regained consciousness, he was adamant that he had been mauled by an enormous, black pig.

Over several days that followed, the guards were terrified and refusing to man certain posts, several having claimed they had witnessed the ghostly image of a black pig around the gaol.

Hysteria began to take hold and the guards and inmates firmly began to believe that the spectral creature was Olocher, his suicide and heinous crime transforming him into a demonic entity. They began to call him 'The Dolocher' and lived in fear of vengeance and retribution.

The area of the prison that seemed to be host to the majority of the alleged demonic activity was near Cork Street and guards were still refusing to take sentry duty. One man volunteered, dismissing the commotion and stories and so began to man his post for the night.

The following morning the brave guard was missing from his post, his rifle and clothes all that remained. It was firmly supposed that Olocher had returned in the form of a Black Pig and that The Dolocher had carried out his first murderous act of vengeance.

The following morning a woman claimed to have been attacked in Christ Church by a Black Pig on the same night the guard went missing, alleging the animal had tried to bite her, but she had run away.

This was just the beginning – night after night throughout The Liberties, a working-class area of Dublin at the time, screams were heard and terrified women were being attacked by The Dolocher, who would then disappear into the night.

The authorities and residents of The Liberties lived in fear and dread, with the winter streets being deserted from nightfall. As the days grew longer and Spring turned to Summer, the attacks ceased, and Dublin began to rest easy.

That was until the dark, foggy nights returned along with The Dolocher. Attacks increased and were more severe, including the savage beating of a pregnant woman who lost her unborn baby.

A group of vigilantes, riled after a night in the tavern recounting the terrible events, took to the streets, killing every pig in sight – and there were many in the city.

The next morning there were no swine carcasses to be found, increasing the fear and terror of the people of Dublin who believed The Dolocher was sent back from Hell and would not rest without retribution.

One particularly nasty night, filled with torrential rain, a blacksmith was finishing up his pint in a tavern in the city and had to walk home. The landlord's wife lent him her large cloak complete with widow's hood to keep him as dry as possible on his travels.

As he walked through The Liberties, he became aware of footsteps and snarling behind him as a creature with the face of a black pig, but the stature of a man set upon him.

The blacksmith was well able to handle himself and soon the menace was lying at his feet. The noise of the brawl had men running from their homes and other taverns and they continued to beat the creature they firmly believed was the demonic creature they called The Dolocher.

When the police arrived at the scene, they discovered not a demon, but a man at death's door who had been wearing the head and skin of a black pig.

At the hospital, they exposed the attacker as the missing sentry from Black Dog Prison. He confessed that he had planned every step, from assisting Olocher with his suicide, to starting the stories of The Dolocher and arranging his own disappearance, so that he could attack innocent women in the guise of a black pig, thinking hysteria would give way to the belief of a supernatural assailant.

The guard also confessed to masterminding the vigilante assault on the swine and clearing away the carcasses during the night. His motive? Robbery pure and simple.

The vicious and nasty mugger died from the injuries inflicted upon him. Some say justice was served, others that another evil felon had escaped the gallows. Either way, The Dolocher was no more.

It is interesting to note that The Liberties of Dublin was an area very much like Whitechapel at the time of Jack the Ripper, a monster who also prayed on women under the cover of night. The Dolocher however was exactly 100 years before Jack the Ripper.

Was it a coincidence? Did Jack get the idea for the Whitechapel murders from the events in Dublin a century before? Just maybe the guard had been possessed by the damned and vengeful spirit of Olocher, a man convicted of the rape and murder of a woman - and maybe that same evil entity took possession of the soul of the man who became known throughout the world as Jack the Ripper.

Never Hostage to the Devil or the Roman Catholic Church – Who Was Father Malachi Martin?

Perhaps one of the most famous names to come out of the Vatican, the former Jesuit priest, best-selling author and professional Exorcist was as well known as a scholar as he was for his outspoken writings and speeches against certain teachings and practices of the Roman Catholic Church.

A writer of both novels and non-fiction and the subject of many rumours himself, sometimes the lines between fact and fiction were blurred – so just who was Malachi Martin and what role did he play in the Vatican's battle against evil and satanic influence.

Malachi Martin was born into a fairly well to do family in the village of Ballylongford just outside of Listowel in County Kerry, Ireland in 1921. Despite claims in later years that Malachi was of Jewish descent, his parents were in fact English and Irish. There were four boys in total and all of them went on to join the priesthood.

The young Malachi entered the Jesuit Order at the age of eighteen after completing his senior education in Dublin. Although further travels and studies were preferred, the outbreak of the Second World War put paid to that and Malachi remained in Ireland, obtaining degrees in Semitic Languages and Oriental Studies.

Once it became safe to travel, the scholar continued his education in Europe with postgraduate studies in several areas including Intertestamentary Studies and education in Hebrew and Arabic Manuscripts. By 1954, Malachi Martin was a fully ordained Jesuit priest.

Always wanting to learn more, Malachi continued to research in the Middle East, including emphasis on the Dead Sea Scrolls and Semitic Palaeography, a study of the methods and context of ancient Middle Eastern writings and scripts.

It was at this time that the young priest found himself assisting on his very first Exorcism in Egypt in the mid-1950s.

Father Martin long believed, had studied, witnessed evidence of the Roman Catholic Church's involvement on a covert level with satanic worship, and was not shy to publish his findings, both in non-fiction and loosely veiled fiction writing.

General knowledge of the dark side of the Church goes back to Pope Benedict IX from the 11th century and his notorious papacy – known to have embraced satanic worship and the black arts, this pope committed atrocities that led to his temporary banishment from Rome. It may well be that he was possessed by the very demons that our 20th Century Exorcist feared.

Even though being a Freemason is forbidden in the Roman Catholic Church, Malachi gave credence to the belief that there were at least two popes involved in the secret sect and that the Illuminati had infiltrated the Vatican. He also believed that nuns were partaking in rituals associated with dark witchcraft.

The young man from a small village in Ireland had come to the attention of the Pope and the Vatican with his prolific studies, dedication and involvement in exorcisms. In 1958, he was called to Rome and took up the position of private secretary to Cardinal Bea, a biblical scholar and a mediator for Catholic-Jewish relations – a mantel Malachi would also take on.

With apartments in the Vatican, the scholarly Father Martin also took the position of Professor of Aramaic, Palaeography, Hebrew and Sacred Scripture at the Pontifical Biblical Institute. Malachi's vast knowledge and diplomacy brought him into contact with many other faiths as an interpreter, from relationships formed with prominent Rabbis to work behind the Iron Curtain with the Russian Orthodox Church.

By 1964, Malachi Martin was on a different path and his traditional approach caused him to be at odds with the outlines laid out by the Second Vatican council. In February of 1965, Father

Malachi Martin was released from his vows of poverty, and finally released from the Jesuit Order in June of the same year.

Brian Doran released an audio account of the life of Malachi Martin told through second hand accounts by those who knew the man called '*God's Messenger*' – according to Doran, Pope Paul VI had "*given the priest a general commission for exercising an apostolate in media and communications.*"

Once Malachi Martin arrived in the United States, he turned his hand to writing and applied for the Guggenheim Fellowship in 1967. This was a grant awarded to the successful applicant for "*demonstrated exceptional capacity for productive scholarship or exceptional creative ability in the arts.*"

Malachi was awarded the grant and this lead to the launch of his first successful book in 1969, '*The Encounter: Religion in Crisis.*' This was Martin's views on why Christianity, Judaism and Islam were in crisis and had failed the modern man.

Following this success, Malachi Martin was awarded the Guggenheim Fellowship for a second time which enabled the priest to write his most famous published work, which went to press in 1975. That book was '*Hostage to the Devil: The Possession and Exorcism of Five Living Americans.*'

Malachi Martin became a U.S Citizen in 1970 and by the end of his life has published some sixty times including thinly veiled insights into the satanic rites of the Vatican with novels such as '*Windswept House: A Vatican Novel*' and a description of the '*Enthronement of the Fallen Angel of Lucifer.*' When asked in an interview with '*The New American*' Martin stated these things had happened but could only be published in a novel.

In 1981, Malachi published '*The Decline and Fall of the Roman Church*', which was a historical volume that focused on the changes through the years and the shifts between progressive supremacy and spiritualism.

Despite having spent more than a quarter of a century as an ordained priest of the Jesuit Order, in 1987 Martin published '*Jesuits: The Society of Jesus and the Betrayal of the Roman Catholic Church.*' This was an inflammatory and extremely critical view of his former brethren and how he believed they destabilised the teachings of the Roman Catholic Church methodically and deliberately.

With so much controversy and celebrity status (Martin was a regular on radio shows and published interviews along with his books) the rumour mill surrounding both him and his own opinions was in overdrive.

Malachi Martin had publicly stated that he believed at least two popes of the 20th century, Pope Pius XI and Pope John Paul 1 were murdered.

Several mysteries surrounded Malachi himself, including whether or not he was actually ordained a bishop. He was also accused among other things of being a spy for the Israelis due to his Jewish sympathising and a story was given of him having Jewish heritage, which was proved to be false.

He was a staunch advocate of the Three Secrets of Fatima. These were three secrets allegedly revealed to three cousins in Portugal over six visits between May and October of 1917. The secrets were:

1. The admission of the existence and description of Hell.
2. Information regarding the First and Second World Wars.
3. The attempted assassination of Pope John Paul 11.

These secrets have been disputed for decades and it is believed they were never revealed in full. Malachi Martin also discredited the religious site of Medjugorje, claiming his previous accreditation was given after being misled. There were also rumours regarding books he may have written under pseudonyms, with at least one being proven.

In a strange twist the notorious serial killer David Berkowitz, known as the Son of Sam, initially claimed on arrest to have been possessed by a demon, however revealed this to be false during meetings with a court psychiatrist. Later while in prison, the convicted Son of Sam actually made approaches to Malachi Martin to assist in writing his autobiography, which Martin declined.

According to Malachi Martin, he had performed thousands of what he referred to as minor exorcisms and participated in a few hundred major exorcisms in his lifetime. As well as private exorcisms, he had worked with renowned Demonologist, Dave Considine and paranormal researcher, John Zaffis.

Perhaps one of the most forthright and knowledgeable authorities on exorcism, Malachi Martin stated that a person cannot unknowingly be possessed or taken against their will, they must actively allow a possession. He believed it to be a systematic and gradual deception by the entity.

Malachi described the process of exorcism as a confrontation between the wills of the exorcist and the demon. In order to succeed, the exorcist has to be empowered by God, through the Church, and have a cleansed soul by way of confession. The process would usually involve the exorcist and an assisting priest, with lay people used for restraining purposes when required.

Father Martin was adamant there were different levels of possession from partial or normal to total where *"... a veil is drawn aside, and you realise you don't know this person. They have a truly evil look."*

He also made it clear that the retelling in film of exorcisms was not as dramatic but there would be temperature drops, bad odours and occasional manifestations. He revealed to Donna Anderson of the Examiner, the worst part was:

"... at a certain moment, if it's really in the possession of a threatening spirit, a demon, everyone will know there's something in the room that wants you dead. It's a horrible feeling knowing that unless something happens you are going to die now. It's like an invisible animal with claws and it want you dead."

Malachi continued to be vocal in his opposition to the Jesuit teachings and aspects of the Vatican as well as insisting that Black Masses and Satanism and sacrifice were happening even within a stone's throw from his residence in New York.

In July 1999, Martin had an alleged fall at his apartment in Manhattan, which led to a cerebral haemorrhage and his death at the age of seventy-eight. Even now, conspiracy theorists believe his fall was not accidental and he was in fact killed by the Vatican to silence his outspoken opposition. Indeed, when questioned during an interview if he feared for his life, he stated he was, however, he was too old to change.

It has been several years since the death of this remarkable man and his books continue to be of major interest among scholars, conspiracy theorists and paranormal researchers to name a few.

His legacy will continue as Marty Stalker, a filmmaker from Northern Ireland has taken Martin Malachi's most famous book, *'Hostage to the Devil'* and made it into a film of the same title.

which includes the use of archive footage. With new media attention and continuing paranormal interest, Malachi Martin will continue to be studied and remembered for decades to come.

I shall leave you with a final word from Malachi Martin:

"Anybody who is acquainted with the state of affairs in the Vatican in the last 35 years is well aware that the prince of darkness has had and still has his surrogates in the court of St. Peter in Rome."

Bridget Cleary – Slaying of a Faery Changeling or Murder?

In 1895, Ireland witnessed the most chilling and compelling of murder trials to ever take place in the Emerald Isle, to the extent it was reported in newspapers throughout Britain, Ireland and Canada. Those charged with her murder cited the Faeries as their defence.

Bridget Boland Cleary was an attractive confident woman of twenty-six years of age. She was married to Michael, an educated Cooper, nine years her senior and the childless couple resided with Bridget's father Patrick Boland in a cottage in Ballyvadlea, County Tipperary.

Bridget was fiercely independent and uncharacteristic of a married woman at that time, as not only was she literate; she was also a very successful businesswoman. A seamstress with her own machine, she made and repaired garments for locals as well as selling eggs from her own chickens. To quote the Judge in the case, Bridget Cleary was "a young married woman, suspecting no harm, guilty of no offence, virtuous and respectable in all her conduct and all her proceedings."

Early in March of that year Bridget had been out delivering eggs and having caught a cold, it escalated, and she became quite ill. The young wife had been subjected to forced intake of herbal concoctions as was the way in that household, however as her condition remained unimproved, the doctor was sent for on the 11th of March, but was unable to attend until the 13th. At this point rumours believed to have been started by Michael and her Uncle Jack

Dunne were circulating the community, stating that Bridget Cleary was gone and that a Faery Changeling had been left in her stead.

On examination the doctor said that Bridget was in a "state of nervous excitement" and had a complaint, possibly TB or Bronchitis. In general, her life was not believed to be at risk. However, the priest was called for to deliver the Last Rites. The priest carried out a last confession and the Last Rites. He too was convinced Bridget was not dying and stated there was no need for him to return.

At this stage, both Michael Cleary and Bridget's father Patrick were openly denouncing the poor woman as a Changeling as she remained sickly. The herbal and folklore 'cures' being administered were becoming more frequent and more brutal. More family and neighbours were now involved and Bridget was subjected to force feeding, urine being thrown upon her as well as being verbally and physically abused. On 14 March, she was finally carried by all present to the fireplace whereupon it was demanded she recite her name three times to prove she was not a Changeling, whilst being held over the fire. On the 16th of March, Bridget Cleary was reported missing.

Michael Cleary stated his wife had been taken by the Faeries and they were seen to be holding a vigil for her safe return. Following intervention from the local priest, after five days Bridget Cleary's corpse was found, buried in a shallow grave, charred and burned.

The horror of her final moments was revealed in court. Nine people in total, with Michael Cleary being the main accused, were charged with her murder and/or wounding. Bridget had been subjected to torture and torment, finally being burned alive in her nightdress in front of the kitchen fireplace, screams of agony ignored by the silent people that stood before her.

That silence continued until arrests were made and the trial began. The evidence brought out at trial was horrific, particularly the post-mortem findings including exposed bones, strangulation marks and burning. Cleary's argument? "She was too fine to be my wife and two inches taller." On this basis, he deduced she was a Changeling and should be slain.

In total five people were convicted, four of wounding and Michael Cleary of the manslaughter of his wife, Bridget Cleary, for which he served 15 years in prison after which time he emigrated.

Was this a clever, jealous husband who convinced his neighbours and family to commit atrocities through mass hysteria?

Did Michael Cleary genuinely believe his wife had been taken by the Faeries? The outcome of the trial points to the former, yet we will never know. All we know is that poor Bridget will forever be remembered as the victim of Ireland's most bizarre and controversial murder trial.

Bridget Cleary's legacy is a nursery rhyme that epitomises the complexity of the circumstances surrounding her death:

Are you a witch or are you a faery?
Or are you the wife of Michael Cleary?

The Murder of 'The Colleen Bawn'

Born into a Limerick farming family in 1803, Ellen Hanley's life was snuffed out in a cold, calculated murder at only 15 years of age.

Living in the village of Bruree, Ellen's mother passed away when the girl was no more than six years old and she moved in with her uncle. Ellen grew into a young lady of incredible beauty that was equally matched by her warmth, quick wit and intelligence.

It was not long before she courted the interest of a certain gentleman of distinction by the name of John Scanlan, John himself was in his twenties and very much a socialite of shallow persuasion which would ultimately lead to Ellen's bitter end.

John Scanlan pursued Ellen relentlessly and begged for her hand in marriage. Ellen had grave misgivings about both the age gap and their different social standing, but John would not take no for an answer. In the summer of 1819, John Scanlan and Ellen Hanley were wed in Limerick city.

True to his form, John grew bored of his child wife within just five weeks of marriage and began to hatch a plot to make her disappear, so he could renew his carefree, lewd lifestyle.

John and his servant Stephen Sullivan schemed and ultimately planned the murder of the new bride. John Scanlan convinced Ellen to take a boating trip on the River Shannon with his servant, leaving from the shores of Glin Castle. Sullivan boarded the boat complete with loaded musket and murder in his heart, however when the time came he was unable to shoot the innocent beauty.

When John Scanlan saw the boat return to Glin with two people on board he was outraged. He filled Stephen Sullivan with whiskey until he was so drunk he agreed to go ahead with the murder plot. Once again, Sullivan rowed Ellen out into the Shannon Estuary and with the threatening words of his master ringing in his ears; the callous servant shot Ellen point blank.

Without an ounce of remorse, Stephen Sullivan stripped Ellen Hanley naked and took her wedding ring, stowing them away in the boat. She was weighed down with rocks and her young, broken body was dropped unceremoniously overboard. Fifteen-year-old Ellen Hanley was enshrouded in the inky black waters of the River Shannon.

Scanlan and Sullivan toasted their successful murder as weeks had passed and they were convinced they had got away with their heinous deed. This was not to be as on the 6th of September 1819, the porcelain white corpse of the missing Ellen was washed up in Kilrush, County Clare.

So horrific was the discovery of the slain child bride, the people of County Clare and County Limerick became frenzied in anger and dismay and the two guilty men fled. A huge manhunt was begun and before long, John Scanlan was captured. The Scanlan family were a family of high standing in social circles and they were not having their name dragged through the mud. They hired the great Irishman Daniel O'Connell, known as 'The Liberator' for his work to bring emancipation to Irish Catholics in later years.

With his family name and the best barrister in Ireland behind him, John Scanlan sat smugly through his trial fully expecting to be acquitted. He could not have been more mistaken.

Scanlan was found guilty without question of the pre-mediated murder of Ellen Hanley. A horse-drawn carriage was commissioned to take the condemned man to Gallows Green in County Clare. The horse bucked and refused to cross the bridge over to Gallows Green and John Scanlan made his last living steps walking to the gallows to be hanged. John Scanlan was executed on 16th March 1820.

The story does not end here, for just a few months later, manservant Stephen Sullivan was caught, and his Limerick trial made front page news. He also was find guilty and sentenced to execution.

In a last-minute fit of conscience, Sullivan recounted the events surrounding the murder of Ellen before the Hangman placed the noose around his fated neck.

In the small, rural Burrane Cemetery near Kilrush the body of the Colleen Bawn, Ellen Hanley is buried. Colleen Bawn is Irish for 'white girl'.Ellen lies beneath a Celtic Cross donated by the local community with an epitaph that says:

'Here lies the Colleen Bawn
Murdered on the Shannon
July 14th 1819. R.I.P'

Over time, the curious and the ghoulish have chiselled away the Celtic Cross bit by bit taking morbid keepsakes until nothing much more remains. The story of the Colleen Bawn lives on almost two hundred years after her untimely death in plays, novels and musical interpretations. It seems that the macabre nature of her demise will never be forgotten.

PHOTOS

Haunted Tapestry Room, Loftus Hall (Dominic McElroy)

Leap Castle (Dominic McElroy)

Silhouette of the Hellfire Club, Dublin (Dominic McElroy)

Kinnitty Castle, County Offally (Ann Massey O'Regan)

CREATURES OF THE FAIRY REALM

Changelings – The Darker Side of Irish Faery Lore

Come away, O human child!
To the waters and the wild
With a faery, hand in hand,
For the world's more full of weeping than you can understand.
(Excerpt from *'The Stolen Child'* by W.B Yeats)

Written about by renowned poets such as Yeats and William Allingham, and used as a defence for murder in the 1800s, mothers for generations in Ireland have been protecting their small ones from abduction, not from humans but from the fairies who replaced them with Changelings, known as *Beácán* (*bay-cawn*). According to legend, abductions took place to increase the strength of faery stock as their own often died during birth and red blood was required in order for the faeries to get into heaven.

The faeries would swap a sickly faery known as the Changeling for the child, whom they would resemble. The Changeling would be recognisable due to an ugly appearance, ill health, bad temper and an old world look of knowledge in their eyes.

There were many protections and deterrents against such abduction. Fireside tongs were laid across the cradle as fairies were thought to be afraid of iron. Red garments were laid in the cradle as these reminded faeries of their fate and Day of Judgement and so were avoided. Crucifixes were hung over cribs like mobiles. Babies were sprinkled with Holy Water to gain God's protection. They were splashed with urine, as faeries did not like unclean babies. Boys would be dressed as girls and vice versa to confuse the faery folk.

For a parent to see if their child had been swapped for a faery, they would leave a set of pipes at their side as no faery can resist playing them and thus their identity would be revealed.

If all the deterrents failed and families were left with a Changeling, there were two options. The first was to threaten its well-being, such as leaving it unattended outside the door. The reasoning was that the faeries remained protective of their own and to avoid any chance of harm they simply returned the child to its parents and took their own back. The second was to keep the faery, which would wither and die within a couple of years if action wasn't taken.

It was believed that if you felt there was no likelihood of the return of your child and you could not bear to raise the Changeling, you could be rid of it by way of burning. Methods included leaving it in the open fire, feeding it foxglove tea to burn internally, or scooping the faery up on a red-hot shovel and leaving it on a manure heap.

The danger is of course, that lore and legend can be deemed as fact or they can be used to try to excuse one's own heinous crime. Indeed, one of Ireland's most written about and strangest murders was that of Bridget Cleary, a young woman who was accused of being a Changeling and was tortured to death by her own family in the late nineteenth century. Bridget was y burned over the fire as her husband wanted to be rid of the Changeling he alleged her to be. Of course, she may not have been a Changeling at all but a victim of a *Piseóg* - however that's a story for next time...

Fairy Shock Troop

When you think of Irish Faeries, or *Sidhe,* as they are known, your imagination probably conjures up images of helpful, shy creatures blessing you with good fortune and this could be your undoing. Irish people know that the *Sidhe* can be very mischievous and demand reverence, but at their worst? Well that's a dark path I will take you down – if you dare.

It has long been believed that the fairy folk are descendants of the Celtic gods and goddesses and the *An Sluagh Sidhe* are no exception. Also known as, 'The Fairy Shock Troop' and 'Fairy Host', these beings are to be deeply feared.

For centuries, they were believed to be the evil souls of the restless departed, rejected by the Celtic gods for their sins and damned to hover between realms, only to venture abroad when the veil between worlds is at its thinnest. These ethereal malevolent creatures are full of anger and vicious in nature, determined to torment and destroy any human who dares to stand in their way.

Essentially warriors, they are always hostile and ready to do battle with any rival host who they encounter. Obsessed with strength, power and splendour, the shock troop will do whatever it takes to maintain their standards and ensure their survival. In the event one of their own are sickly or impaired, they will abduct a human, usually a gifted child who has great beauty and strength.

The *An Sluagh Sidhe* travel through the air, reaping havoc as they fly. It is believed that many sailors and fishermen have lost their lives as the fury of the host creates a tempest, reducing boats to kindling and casting those on board into the icy seas and rivers.

When roaming over land a whirlwind is created by the *An Sluagh Sidhe* called the *Gaoithe Sidhe* (Faery Wind), which is heralded by a an ominous droning that vibrates through to your very soul. Farmers caught in their fields would pray in desperation as they watched it come towards them, helpless to defend themselves or their crops and cattle.

The *Gaoithe Sidhe* could rip the roof from the strongest homestead, allowing the faery troop to get inside and carry a soul away. Magic gusting forth from the tornado of devastation would strike musicians daring to play fairy music and leave them silent, destroy crops and damage the sight of animals and humans who were unable to escape its wrath.

If you were unfortunate enough to be caught in the path of the fairy wind, you would hit with a '*Poc si*' ,or fairy stroke, that blighted fields and was believed to be responsible for ailments and deformities. Children in its wake were left unable to grow further and if you pulled a face at the oncoming host, the wind would blow, and your features would remain forever crooked.

The only way to be protected from the might of the *An Sluagh Sidhe* is to throw iron into the oncoming squall. Should you hear a piercing scream you know you have hit your mark and must shout 'May my misfortune go with you!' This should shield you as they pass over, however, be sure to be far away from their path upon the next visit. The Fairy Shock Troop will not forget and have an eternity to exact their revenge. If you hear the drone of bees and feel a gust of wind at your neck, run. Don't look back - the fairy wind is approaching carrying the ruthless Fairy Shock Troop and they're coming for you.

Cait Sidhe

There is one tale that is definitely more rooted in Scottish Folklore than Irish yet still features in tales from both sides of the water. The Cait *Sidhe* or *Cait Sith* is inscrutable and very little is known although there is more to glean from Scottish lore. The creature seems to stem from the Highlands of Scotland yet pops up in exactly the same form in Irish culture.

The fairy being is in the shape of a large black cat with a white spot and is believed to be a soul reaper. Traditions include putting out fires so as not to entice the *Cait Sidhe* with heat and distracting it from the body of the recently deceased with games and puzzles.

On the feast of Samhain, many homes would leave out milk so that the *Cait Sidhe* would bless the home for the coming year. Those who didn't would be cursed and the milk from their cows would run dry.

One explanation of the existence of the *Cait Sidhe* is that it is a witch. It is said that certain witches have the ability to transform into a feline up to eight times while retaining the ability to change back. Should the witch decide to change a ninth time, she is destined to stay in that form of the forever. Perhaps why a cat is said to have nine lives.

A Guide to Leprechauns

We've all seen them in film and television from *Leprechaun* to *Darby O'Gill and the Little People* and have no doubt worn the St. Patrick's Day T- Shirt, but what do you really know about Leprechauns? Here's a beginner's guide to Ireland's most recognisable and smallest inhabitant.

Origins

Around for over 1000 years, the leprechaun is descended from the supernatural race known as Tuatha Dé Danann and are a part of the

Sidhe or Fairy family. The name Leprechaun has two sources, both from old Irish. The first is *Leath Bhrogan*, meaning shoemaker and the second is *Luacharma'n* meaning small body. Made infamous by the likes of Yeats and Allingham, the once hidden and little-known leprechauns are a symbol of Ireland the world over.

Appearance

No more than three feet high, leprechauns are proportionately stocky in build.   They have wizened, aged faces, almost grotesque in appearance, save for their mischievous, fiery eyes.   Although stereotyping has them dressed head to toe in green, leprechaun clothing includes red and brown outfits and different styles of hat. The two things they are never without are a pipe known as a dudeen full of foul smelling tobacco and a jug under the arm full of beer or poteen.

Activities

Leprechauns like to keep themselves to themselves and really don't like mortals - or each other. Very much loners they are happiest in their own intoxicated company, their only friend being the robin - probably because it won't ask to share. They are gainfully employed as shoemakers, distillers and as bankers for the otherworld, the latter of which leaves them in a permanent state of anxiety as they struggle to keep the crocks of fairy gold hidden from mortals and other thieving hands.   Constantly moving the hoard around, they are followed by rainbows, the end of which is the equivalent of 'X' marks the spot for those looking for fairy treasure.   Much like mortal bankers, the pressure of work, constantly moving money around to avoid being found and trying to keep up a certain lifestyle takes its toll and leads to alcohol dependency.

Varieties

There are no female leprechauns and if you ask a leprechaun how they reproduce you are bound to get a swift kick in the shins for your trouble. There are however several types:

<u>Clurichaun</u>– This jolly, ruddy faced creature is very partial to a drop of the good stuff and any wine cellar or drinks store is in for a world of ruin if one takes residence. He works hard all day and really lets his hair down at night, riding dogs and sheep for the craic. If you give him a bottle and make him welcome, you will be protected. Don't however, insult or anger the Clurichaun or you will pay. He is recognised by silver buckles on his shoes, blue stockings and gold laces in a cap made of leaves. Also known as 'His Nibs'.

<u>Leinster Leprechaun</u> – The least ostentatious of all the leprechauns, the Leinster fellow keeps a low profile and is distinguished from other leprechauns due to his love of honey.

<u>Ulster Leprechaun</u> – The Tom Cruise of the leprechauns, he wears built up heels on his shoes and a pointy hat to make himself look taller. A talented poet and an accomplished hurler, what the Ulster wee man doesn't have in height he makes up for in skill.

<u>Meath Leprechaun</u> – A born diplomat, the Meath leprechaun has no need to kiss the Blarney Stone. As a result of this he loves the sound of his own voice and will happily use a hundred words where ten will do. Don't rush him along though, this will antagonise him and he will let you know – at length.

<u>Connaught Leprechaun</u> – Hardworking, Industrious and very reclusive, keeps his head down and only enjoys a tipple when his work is done.

<u>Munster Leprechaun</u> – The most extrovert of the bunch, he is a wild party animal. Munster Leprechaun is known for his legendary drinking habits. When sober he has the most amiable character, but once the drink is inside him, watch out!

<u>Fear Dearg (Red Man)</u> - Recognised by his blemished yellowy skin, Fear Dearg is dressed head to foot in red and is known for mischief, mockery and pranks. His greatest delight is your fear and dread. If you don't mind the Red Man he will destroy your livelihood, home and health in a heartbeat.

Wishes and Curses.

The story of the leprechaun and three wishes can be traced back to the time of Fergus mac Léti, King of Ulster. Legend has it that Fergus fell asleep on the shore and our little friends attempted to drag him into the sea. The cold water woke him and he seized them in his hands. Fearing for their lives, they offered the king three wishes in exchange for their freedom. One of Fergus mac Léti's wishes was for the ability to be able to breathe under water, which would lead to his demise.

No good comes from a leprechaun's wishes! My advice? If you catch one of the little blackguards, let him go. If he doesn't charm you, he'll harm you. On the other hand, if you don't offer a leprechaun hospitality when he seeks it, particularly the red man, you will be cursed to your very soul!

Leprechauns have survived for millennia due to their solitary and resourceful nature and will no doubt be around long after we have departed this mortal coil. By all means, wear the t-shirts and don the hats and beards for St. Patrick's Day, but don't let them catch you as they are proud and easily offended – and don't think for a second you will ever get the better of one or steal its guarded treasure, as a lifetime is a long time for a leprechaun to gleefully torment you in revenge.

Merrow- Seducers of the Irish Seas

Since the time of the Ancient Greeks, there have been folktales of oceanic Femme Fatales luring men to an early grave. These maidens of the sea have proven as lethal as they are beautiful, and the Irish mermaid known as the 'Merrow', is no exception.

The name derives from the old Irish '*Moruadh*' meaning 'sea maid'. Although the literal translation is feminine, the term Merrow applies to both the male and female of the species. They are said to dwell in '*Tir fo Thoinn*', or 'the Land beneath the waves'.

Merrow Men

Merrow menfolk really don't have a lot going for them. They are hideously ugly to the point that the mermaids refuse to take them as a mate, despite their genetic compatibility.

There is actually very little documented about these loathsome creatures, however they have been described in stories as being covered in emerald scales with a stunted body and limbs. They have green course hair, grotesque pointed teeth and bloodshot eyes. Merrow men are so bitter over their appearance and loneliness, that they capture the spirits of drowned sailors and keep them incarcerated under the sea in a desperate attempt at revenge.

Merrow Women

Merrow women on the contrary, are absolutely striking. They have long, radiant hair and from the waist down, have glistening verdigris scales covering a quite remarkable fish tail. The beauty of the Merrow takes the breath of men away figuratively and literally. Their exquisite singing can mean either harmonious joy or death to those who succumb to the melodic enchantment.

Many human males have been seduced over time into mating with the female Merrow. Those with the Irish surnames of as O'Flaherty and O'Sullivan in County Kerry and MacNamara in County Clare are believed to descend from such unions. Of course, such relations were short-lived as the mermaid would become homesick for her subterranean way of life and would drag her suitor beneath the water.

Poor unsuspecting men would be enticed into the sea by the bewitching music of the Merrow women and be pulled beneath the waves to live in entranced captivity. In the event one absconded, they would incur the wrath of the scorned Siren and be hunted and then drowned. If an escaped prisoner *really* antagonised their captor they would be angrily devoured, bones and all.

Written accounts of the Merrow women luring unsuspecting Irishmen date back to the ancient Annals of the Kingdom of Ireland, also known as the Annals of the Four Masters. Indeed, even the all-powerful demi-gods of chaos known as the Fomorians were not immune to their charms.

The Formorians and the Merrow

Roth was a Fomorian son carrying out his duties patrolling the coastal borders of Ireland. It would appear that the Merrows took umbrage at his presence within their seas and took steps to ensure he would no longer pose a threat. The seemingly innocent beauties of the waters began their attack by lulling Roth gently to sleep with their enchanting melodies.

Once he was sedated and clearly unable to fight back, they became bloodthirsty and homicidal. Violently they tore the poor misfortune limb from limb and joint from joint. Although much of him was consumed, the creatures sent his thigh floating over the current, the jagged femur pointing to what has now become known as the county of Waterford.

Of course, sometimes on a bad day there didn't need to be a catalyst to stir up the wrath and destruction of these ill-tempered wily sea maids. They would simply take pleasure in brewing up storms, shipwrecking and drowning innocent sailors for no other reason other than crossing their watery path.

Luty Of County Kerry and the Merrow

County Kerry lies on the Atlantic coast of Ireland and has strong links to the Merrow folk. Stories date back centuries and the most famous one of all involved a gentle fisherman who would rue the day he ever set eyes upon a Merrow woman.

Whilst walking on the beach, a young man by the name of Luty saw an incredible sight. There, lying on the shingle was the most beautiful female he had ever seen. A woman in every way bar her fish tail that was floundering on the sand.

His kind nature took over from the disbelief and he realised quickly that the creature before him was in terrible distress. He lifted the woman into his two strong arms and carried her out to the waves. The Merrow was named Marina and she was so ecstatic at being rescued, her malicious nature was subdued and she granted Luty three wishes.

He asked for the ability to break curses brought about by dark magic, to be able to command malevolent spirits to carry out charitable deeds and the power to make good things happen for those in need. The young man's selflessness impressed the sea-maiden so much she added a final gift of prosperity to Luty and all his future descendants.

Luty was delighted and reached out to shake her hand. Sensing the pureness of his soul, her true wickedness came to the forefront and she began to seduce the unsuspecting hero with her alluring voice. A shocked Luty realised almost immediately what she was doing and reached into his pocket for his iron knife.

As with all fairy folk, Marina could be harmed with iron and he lashed out. The mermaid dived beneath the waves but not before uttering a terrifying promise to come back and reclaim Luty in nine years. Time passed and Luty married a local girl and had two sons. He took his youngest son fishing and as Luty reached the shore, Marina rose from the ocean depths and grabbed the poor misfortune, dragging him down into the angry waves and he was never heard from again.

Protection from the Merrow

The Merrow wear a special enchanted cap called a *cohuleen druith*. The garment and indeed the Merrow penchant for capturing the souls of hapless sailors was spoken of in the nineteenth century Thomas Keightley book of folk tales, *The Soul Cages*. The *cohuleen druith* holds the power of the Merrow that enables them to live under the ocean.

If you are fast enough to snatch it from the head of the siren before she enchants you, she is no longer able to descend beneath the waves and she is very much at your mercy. Of course, if you are too late and your senses are ensnared – well I am afraid you are doomed to an eternity in a soul cage, trapped at the bottom of the sea.

Seduction & Destruction – The Lure of the Gancanagh

If you wondered why Irish males have a reputation for being smooth talking, tall dark and handsome strangers, then you need look no further than the *Gancanag*h (Gawn-canack). The name has a literal translation of 'Love Talker' and the title is no word of a lie!

One of the solitary fairy folk, the *Gancanagh* is part of the leprechaun family, although you wouldn't think it to look at him. Tall, wiry and very easy on the eye, women are drawn helplessly to this ethereal being before he even begins to weave his intoxicating magic.

Tales of this mystery man stealing hearts and sanity date back over millennia. Likened to the Incubus, the *Gancanagh* is subtler and more deadly. Traditionally his target would be the women of the rural areas such as milkmaids, devouring their chastity and casting shame on the family, but he moves on with the times as much as he does with locations.

He is dressed stylishly and oozes charm with his distinguished pipe or 'dudeen' pressed between his lips. The *Gancanagh* is nonchalant on the surface and appears lazy but don't be fooled. He will charm, lie and ultimately seduce you – once that happens, your deadly fate is sealed.

I may have misled you by painting a romantic picture of this fairy, however this is just the façade. He isn't just looking for love, he is looking for complete control using his intoxicating touch and when his prey is completely dependent he callously withdraws his affection and leaves.

The victims of the *Gancanagh* fall into a lovesick frenzy, and like any drug addiction, it takes over their bodies and minds with disastrous consequences. Isolated from family and friends, pining for the touch of the *Gancanagh*, just spiralling into madness until death becomes a welcome but early release.

In modern culture W.B Yeats referred to the *Gancanagh* as being mysterious and relatively unknown in *Fairy and Folk Tales of the Irish Peasantry* yet he has become known – it is possible that this creature inspired Oscar Wilde to write of Dorian Gray. This enigmatic yet deadly fairy even found himself featured in a Cork based episode of *Murder She Wrote*! There is one way to protect yourself from this seductive creature. An amulet made from the twigs of a rowan and mistletoe, pinned together with an iron nail and bound with a blood-soaked thread.

The Púca

Throughout Europe and probably the world, every country has its own version of the *Púca* (also known as *Pooka, Phouka* and *Phuca)*. In Ireland, it is of the fairy realm, a creature that changes appearance and a most feared and esteemed part of Celtic folklore. *Púca* translates as ghost or spirit, a good description of an evasive yet terrifying dark being who materialises at night throughout the country.

Mostly this shapeshifter will appear in rural areas, particularly on mountains and hills. Seen as many things including a rabbit, in County Down, it is seen as a hideous goblin, demanding a share of the harvest. In County Laois, it is seen as giant hairy bogeyman and in Waterford and Wexford, it is seen as an enormous eagle. In Roscommon, people see the *Púca* as a black goat with large curling horns, but most will say it is a Black Stallion with a wild flowing mane and yellow eyes that burn like sulphur.

The *Púca* is synonymous with the Gaelic festival of Samhain, to mark the bringing in of the harvest and the start of winter. In fact, 1 November, the traditional start of this festival is also known as '*Púca* Day'. It is said that fruit must not be eaten after this day as it has been spat on by the *Púca*, thus bewitching it and making it inedible. After harvesting anything left in the field is considered to be 'puka' or fairy-blasted, meaning it is spoiled and must not be touched. This is left and known as *Púcas* Share.

The 1st of November is believed to be the one day the *Púca* is supposed to be civil. Indeed, if you treat it with reverence you could find it in good humour, giving you warnings or prophecies or even saving you from the malevolent fairies who roam abroad at this time of year. Oscar Wilde's own mother Jane, a poet in her own right and a prolific collector of Irish Fairy Tales believed them to come to the aid of farmers in need. Ask anyone who has encountered the *Púca* however, and they will have a very different story.

The *Púca* in its guise as a Dark Horse will roam the landscape, ochre eyes blazing, tearing down fences and destroying farms. It tramples crops and makes cattle stampede. Its stare will cause cows to stop producing milk and hens to stop laying eggs. The *Púca* has the ability to converse with humans and before its nightly run will call to a house for company. If that company is refused, then the property will be razed to the ground.

Lonely travellers walking country roads have been swept up and thrown onto the back of the wild stallion and taken on a nightlong terrifying ride through the countryside, to be shaken off in the grey light of morning, shaken, no memory of the ride yet changed forever.

One man, weary of having been taken twice was believed to have tricked the *Púca* on the third time by wearing silver spurs and causing it much pain. In return for his dismount the *Púca* agreed to leave him alone.

Only one has succeeded in catching and taming the *Púca*, the High King Brian Boru. He brought the creature to bear by making a bridle using three strands of its mane. In return for its freedom, the *Púca* was made to promise not to harm an Irishman again, unless he was intoxicated or partaking in evil deeds. After some years the notoriously untrustworthy and untruthful tormentor reverted to old tricks, forgetting the promise it had made.

The story of the *Púca* remains very much alive in modern times, being reference in the poems of W.B Yeats and more recently in the films *Harvey* and *Donnie Darko*. Until a short time ago, in South Fermanagh locals would gather in high places to await a speaking horse on Bilberry Sunday. If you were to go looking for one, you should start in Wicklow, in Poulaphuca, which translates as 'The *Púca*'s Hole'.

So, if you were drunk last night and have woken up the worse for wear, mysterious injuries and no memory of events, you might well have been under the spell of the *Púca* – you may have been taken on the ride of your life.

If you find yourself in Ireland travelling alone at night, be wary. If you come across the *Púca* you could be in for the ride of your life!

VAMPIRES, WEREWOLVES AND DEMONS

On the Trail of the Irish Vampire

*The last I saw of Count Dracula was his kissing his hand to me,
with a red light of triumph in his eyes, and with a smile that Judas
in hell might be proud of."*
— **Bram Stoker, Dracula**

For generations there has been a fascination with the vampire,
creature of the night and blood-sucking demon. The origins of such
a demonic entity stretch back to ancient civilisations and trail across
countries and oceans - from Ancient Greeks writing of blood drinking
revenants to current sightings of the South American Chupacabra.

Modern folklore and popular culture have ultimately taken
tales and accounts from 18th Century Europe and created a distinctive,
deadly and dark evil force that has spawned countless best-selling
books, TV shows and films. Transylvania in Romania is recognised
as the number one hotspot for discovering the legend of the Vampire;
however, unknown to many, Ireland has an historic and altogether
dark Vampiric trail of its own dating back to the 5th Century at least!

Abhartach – Vampire Clan Chief

During the 5th Century in what is now known as Derry, the area was
in a constant state of battle between rival clans seeking power and
dominion over one another. The leader of one of these clans was the
cruel and twisted Chieftain Abhartach. His name roughly translates
as dwarf and he was believed to either be such or had several
deformities.

Regardless of either Abhartach was a formidable opponent
and vicious warrior. He was the definition of pure evil and such was
the clan chief's passion for darkness and depravity he was feared as
a powerful and sadistic sorcerer.

So much so in fact, that his own clan cowered in his presence
and plotted his demise. They hired the services of a rival Chieftain
who slew Abhartach and buried him in a solitary grave standing
upright, as was the tradition for warriors of that time.

Celebrations were short-lived however, as a somewhat
disgruntled Abhartach returned from the grave the following night,

demanding fresh blood from his clan to sustain his life. Clan Chief Cathan was both perplexed and furious that his efforts had failed and knew his reputation was at stake. Once again, he killed the dwarf and buried him exactly as before.

In scenes reminiscent of the accounts of Rasputin, it would appear Abhartach was immortal as he returned to his village once again to seek vengeance and drink the blood of his people.

Convinced that Abhartach was indeed wielding some black magic influence, Cathan sought the advice of a Druid Priest and finally cut down the wicked creature with a sword carved from the Yew tree, possibly the most powerful mystical reference for Druids.

Abhartach was interred for the final time head first, never to resurface - or so we are led to believe. In the current area of Derry known as Glenullin, there is a location known as the Giant's Grave, which in itself, is interesting when one thinks of the dwarf Chieftain. It is also known as Abhartach's Sepulchre, or *Leacht Abhartach.* Upon the grave lies a weighty boulder and through it grows a thorn bush, the thorn being another important Druid symbol. If the Vampire Chieftain does indeed lie within, one most hope he does not rise again.

Dearg Due and Vampiric Retribution

Arranged marriages have always been prevalent in Irish culture, particularly to increase power and wealth between families. The story of the Dearg Due is no exception. A girl in Waterford with exceptional beauty was born into such a family.

As fate had it, she was humble and content and sought love in the arms of a local farm hand. They made plans to wed and have a family of their own. Her cruel father however, was fuelled by avarice and prosperity, regardless of the cost to his own kin. He gave his daughter to a notorious vicious and nasty clan Chief in exchange for land and riches.

With the marriage set and the young woman condemned to a life of cruelty, the wedding day she had dreamed of had become a horrific nightmare. On the day of the wedding the reluctant bride was a vision of blinding beauty, dressed in red and gold. As all the guests revelled long into the night, the girl sat alone, angry and bitter -

damning her father to hell and vowing to seek revenge on those who had cost her love and life.

The Chieftain turned out to be far more abusive and controlling then his new wife could ever have imagined. To him the poor girl was nothing but a trophy to be locked away for his pleasure only, savouring the knowledge she was his and his alone. With a complete absence of hope and only darkness ahead, she simply existed – no longer eating or drinking, her life gone long before her body gave in.

Her burial was poorly attended and without ceremony. Her wicked husband had taken another wife before she was even cold, and her family were too engrossed in their wealth and greed to give her a second thought. Only one man grieved for the tragic young woman, her lost love. He visited her grave every single day telling her of his undying love and praying for her return.

Unfortunately, his love was not the driving force for her resurrection – revenge was the force that pulled her from her grave on the first anniversary of her death. Consumed with hatred and the need for retribution she burst from her coffin and headed home. As her father lay sleeping she touched her lips to his and sucked the worthless, selfish life straight out of him.

Revenge not yet sated, she called upon her callous husband finding him surrounded by women, fulfilling his lustful desires, oblivious to the dead bride in the room. In a furious rage, she launched on the Chieftain sending the women screaming. His former wife was so full of fury and fire that she not only drew every breath but drained every ounce of blood from his twisted and cruel body.

The scarlet liquid surging through her, leaving her more alive than she had ever been, and she had a hunger for blood that could not be sated.

The corpse bride used her beauty to prey on young men, luring them to their demise with seduction, the promise of her body their reward. Instead, she sank her teeth into their exposed necks and drank their blood to quench her thirst and desire, but it was never enough. The warm elixir gave her strength and immortality and drove her to her next quarry. That is until the terrified locals restrained her and buried her in a mystical place known as Strongbow's Tree.

The Femme Fatale's lustful yearning can only be satisfied on the day she died, so on the eve of her anniversary locals would gather and place stones upon her grave so that she would not rise and fulfil her blood-lust. Sometimes though the rocks are dislodged, forgotten or her insatiable desire is stronger than any boulder could ever be. That is when she can walk into the night, ill-fated men falling victim to the beauty and bloodthirstiness of the Dearg Due.

Deviants – The Rising of the Dead

The Kilteasheen Archaeological Project was a joint effort between Sligo Institute of Technology and Saint Louis University. They were tasked with searching for a Medieval Bishop's Palace in use until abandonment following the arrival of the Plague in the middle of the 14th century. They began their excavation beneath flagstones in quiet fields in Kilteasheen, County Roscommon in 2005.

The first shock discovery was that directly under the stones were the crushed skeletons of many humans, piled several deep in shallow graves. The shallowness, together with the positioning of the flagstones indicated that the builders knew they were building directly on top of a graveyard containing upwards of to 3000 corpses.

It was further discovered that on the perimeter of the graveyard were two further burial plots. Once excavations began, it became clear that these were no ordinary interments. The deceased had been buried in a manner conducive to what is historically known as a deviant burial. Once the skeletons were revealed, the violent, horrific nature of their post-mortem treatment became clear.

The men had been buried during different time periods. There were no genetic similarities and their ages varied by some twenty or so years; however, they were connected in a most disturbing manner. Each body was subjected to the breakage of arms, legs, hands and feet. These limbs were then folded inwards and bound around a large boulder. Both men had a rock wedged so firmly into his mouth that his jaws were close to snapping apart.

These men were not being laid to rest, they were being grotesquely violated and weighted down to ensure they would not return from the dead. The other interesting observation was that the men had not died of natural causes. Blade marks were clearly visible upon the bones.

In medieval times, it was believed that the mouth was the portal to the soul. By placing an object such as a stone into the mouth of the deceased, the corrupt soul that had departed could no longer return. By breaking and binding the flesh and bones, the deviant could not walk among the living again.

The extent of mutilation together with the stone in the mouth of the dead pointed to one possibility. That the people who carried out these actions believed they were in the presence of vampires. It was believed at first that the archaeological team were on a Black Death site, as it was thought vampires spread plague and the violent nature of the burials was consistent with those thought to be involved in vampirism.

Bone dating however, showed that the corrupt corpses had gone through the most gruesome of rituals centuries before the Black Death took hold. So long before Vampires were written into folklore, before they were romanticised and turned into best-selling stories, the undead were believed to be walking among the Irish, bringing sickness and death to animals and people alike. In a small village in the West of Ireland, locals were using every ritual and method they had to make sure it didn't happen to them. In Kilteasheen, the Deviants would never rise again.

The Dublin Man and the Ultimate Vampire

In 1897, a fifty-year-old Dublin man by the name of Bram Stoker published a book with a simple cover and a simple title. That book was *Dracula*. From humble beginnings, the gothic horror novel was initially met with lukewarm public interest but to great critical acclaim. Like many writers, Stoker was forced to maintain a day job and published his most recognised work during his time as manager of the Lyceum Theatre in London.

The book itself was set between the seaside town of Whitby in England, where Stoker had holidayed, and Eastern Europe, which the writer had never visited. So where did his inspiration come from? After making acquaintance with a Hungarian writer, he became fascinated by the folklore tales from the regions of Eastern Europe and took it upon himself to conduct detailed research into the tales of vampirism from those very localities.

Interestingly however, Stoker was said to have visited Killarney in County Kerry and in particular the ruins of 15th century Muckross Abbey and graveyard. The ruins of the church, cloister and graveyard are well preserved and stand in the shadow of ancient Yew trees.

The site contains a graveyard and was the burial place of local chieftains. Three of Ireland's great poets of the 17th and 18th century are entombed here, which could well be reason behind the famous Irish writer's visit. There are two local accounts that Stoker may well have heard that may have been catalysts for *Dracula* as Stoker was in Killarney prior to the creation of the world's most famous vampire.

The first account is of a religious hermit named John Drake lived in the deserted Friary for more than a decade in the 18th century. He had no worldly goods and slept only in a coffin left in the grounds. The second is the legend of the Brown Man, a newly wed whose bride came looking for him one night, to find her husband knelt over a recently dug up corpse, feasting on its flesh.

With so much in the way of centuries old Irish folklore and legend pertaining to the vampire, together with anecdotes and tales Bram Stoker picked up on his Irish travels, it would not be a far stretch to surmise that this in part contributed to the spark of creation that became Dracula.

The Werewolves of Ossory

In 1182, a priest set out from Ulster to the south of Ireland on official Holy business with his squire. They travelled from morning until dusk, when they moved from the road and into the edge of the forest to seek shelter. As it grew dark, the squire lit a fire as much to protect them from anything lurking in the trees as for warmth, as the priest was on a mission and knew the Devil would be out to try and to lure him from his path.

As the squire slept, the priest sat by the light of the fire, the noises of the forest all around him. He suddenly looked up realising there was no sound, just eerie silence. A snap of a branch startled the priest and he moved closer to the flames as he heard a raspy voice call out, "Father do not be afraid, I mean you no harm."

The priest called back out into the trees "Move into the light my son and I shall have no need to be afraid."

With this, there was some shuffling and the priest squinted into the darkness but could see nothing.   The voice said, "I fear my physical appearance will cause you distress and I do not wish to see you alarmed, I merely seek the help of a Holy man."

The priest replied "My son I have travelled this country and seen the damage and deformity that illness and disease can cause. I will not be alarmed."

A great hulking shape emerged from the still of the night, matted fur, dripping from its jowls, sharp pointed teeth glistening in the light of the fire. The priest was terrified yet stayed calm so as not to cause further anguish to his squire who was now awake and cowering in fear behind a tree. Without a doubt the priest knew before him was a wolf-man. He had heard stories of the same being used as weapons among the Ancient Kings of Ireland as they battled one another.

"Explain yourself and know I am protected by the Lord God," said the priest.

"Father, I too am a Christian. Years ago, my clan were cursed by Abbot Natalis. Every seven years, two of our clan are transformed into werewolves and banished to the forest. When we return after seven years, two more take our place. The sin for which my clan was punished has long been forgotten but we remain cursed."

The priest knew of Natalis and his severe methods of forcing Christianity upon a Pagan land.

The wolf-man continued, "My wife and I were very old on our turning and she now lies wounded and dying in the forest. I beg of you to administer the Last Rites, so she may die a Christian and pass into heaven. "

The priest agreed and leaving his squire behind followed the werewolf into the forest. As they approached a hollow in the trees, the priest could make out the outline of the she-wolf. As he neared he could hear her shallow rasping breaths.

"Help me father and hear my contrition" she begged.

"I want to", said the priest "but first I need proof that you are indeed human under your fur."

With this the she-wolf used her last ounce of strength to tear fur and skin from her front leg and paw so the priest could see she was indeed, a dying old woman. He hurriedly gave her the Last Rites as she died.

The grateful werewolf took the priest back to his squire and the priest promised to call again. He informed his bishop who in turn reported to Rome, documented in 1185. Despite his best efforts, the priest was unable to find the werewolf or his clan again.

The Demon Bride

There are few greater superstitions and fears in Ireland than those associated with death. It comes as no surprise then, to learn of a 'Demon Bride' stealing the life force from ill-fated mourners.

Immortalised in the ballad *Sir Turlough* also known as *The Churchyard Bride* by William Carleton, the story of the Demon Bride has been terrorising funeral goers for at least two hundred years and the bodies of her tragic victims lay buried in the very churchyard where their fate was sealed.

Errigal-Truagh Graveyard in County Monaghan is the location of this malevolent spirit who brings heartbreak to the locals. It is said that the ghoul lies in wait as the deceased are laid to rest and the grievers slowly make their way from the graveside and out of the cemetery, where there is always someone who lingers behind. When that person is a young man, the evil spirit manifests as a beautiful young woman who encapsulates all the desires of the naïve male.

Rousing the ill-fated prey with ardour and yearning, the Demon Bride exacts a promise from the smitten man that he will meet her a month precisely from that day in the very graveyard that they met. She seals the promise with a passionate fiery kiss, sending waves of lust and longing pulsating through his veins, rendering him irresistible to her advances.

The moment the promise has been made by the willing victim the spirit disappears. Dazed and confused, the young man makes his way to the gates of the graveyard and on crossing over its boundary his blood runs cold as comprehension turns to horror and despair. The poor wretch realises he has sold his body and soul for the kiss of an evil spectre and that his life is now forfeit.

As dismay and terror take a hold of his sanity, the unfortunate youth descends in madness, each minute reliving his downfall and awaiting his ultimate demise. One month to the very day of his costly mistake, the crazed young man dies in his own ravings and insanity and is buried in the very place he met the Demon Bride, his promise fulfilled.

Do not think you are safe from this Siren however. If she does not get her quarry in the graveyard, she will attend weddings and other festivities as a bewitching female. Once she has you in her sights, she will have you dance into a frenzy of passion and desire, until your mind is overwhelmed with hysteria and you die exhausted and insane, the Demon Bride's evocative image being the last thing you will ever see.

My advice? Don't be taken in by the mysterious beauty at a wedding and don't ever be the last to leave a funeral – the next one could be yours.

MYSTICAL AND ETHEREAL LOCATIONS

Mystical Skellig Michael – Star Wars and So Much More!

Skellig Michael is one of two islands alongside Small Skellig, which make up the Skellig Islands, reachable by boat from the fishing village of Portmagee in County Kerry. The name derives from the Irish '*Sceillic*', which means 'Steep Rock.'

The name is not misleading as the imposing natural formation stands more than 700 feet above sea level.

Star Wars aside, Skellig Michael is noted for not only incredibly well preserved archaeological sites of interest, but also for the incredible amount of breeding birds it is home to. Rare birds such as gannets, puffins and artic terns draw in Ornithologists from around the globe.

Skellig Michael and the Milesians

The origins of Skellig Michael are shrouded in mystery; however, there are documented accounts of the craggy outpost in ancient texts and annals. One such event dates back to 1700 B.C.

King Milesius spent many years absent from his homeland of Spain in pursuit of greatness and knowledge in places such as Egypt. He was welcomed as a hero upon his return and drove out hostile nations attempting to gain control.

As Spain fell victim to famine, Milesius found himself heavily influenced by the words of Cachear the Druid as well as his own superstitious beliefs. In order to appease the gods and his people, the King ordered members of his family to head up a scouting mission to a green and bountiful land that became known as Ireland.

Although his sons were successful in their conquering of Ireland and Milesius himself came to be known as 'The Father of the Irish Race', the initial expedition party ended in tragedy. The Chief Leader was a son of Milesius, called Ir. Unlike those who followed in his footsteps, Ir was doomed to never set foot on the Irish mainland. During a stormy crossing, his ship crashed with the waves onto the rocks of Skellig Michael and he and his crew were drowned, the unforgiving natural wonder their final resting place.

The Monks of Skellig Michael

Saint Finnian of Clonard, also known as Fionán, was one of Ireland's first monastic saints and he was responsible for the education and training of the Twelve Apostles of Ireland in County Meath in the sixth century.

It is believed that during this time Fionán founded a monastery on Skellig due to its remoteness and isolation from civilization. The actual location of the monastery on the island was selected for durability and access to building materials.

It was sometime between here and the 11th century that the monastery and Church were dedicated to Saint Michael, giving the large rocky habitat its name.

Monks continued to live, work and pray in solitude on Skellig Michael, believing their removal from general society brought them closer to God. Nature had a different opinion however, and as the centuries passed, conditions on the island become intolerable.

In the 1200s, the Order of St. Augustine relocated to Ballinskelligs Abbey; however, Skellig Michael remained under their authority and became a site of pilgrimage until the dissolution of the Catholic Church in Ireland under the command of Queen Elizabeth I of England.

Subsequent History of Skellig Michael

Despite its isolated and hostile demeanor, Skellig Michael was gaining European attention. It was known to the Spanish Armada during their attacks on the Irish Atlantic coastline and was documented on charts and maps of Europe during the Middle Ages.

In 1578, Queen Elizabeth granted the island of Skellig Michael to the Butler Family who maintained control for a further number of generations, until it was purchased by Irish authorities in the 19th century as a matter of maritime safety. It was at this point that not one, but two lighthouses were built to combat the combination of stormy high seas and the perilous rocks that had caused the deaths of so many sailors – too late for Ir!

Skellig Michael Today

Skellig Michael has become a must visit location for naturalists, ornithologists, archaeologists and tourists for decades, who are not deterred by the cantankerous ocean crossing from the Kerry mainland or the intensely steep ascent.

Once there, the remains of the monastery, St. Michael's Church, the Monk's Graveyard and over a hundred crosses dominate the rugged landscape.

In order to ascend to the monastery, one must climb 618 steps where you will stand at more than 600 feet above sea level. The reward far outweighs the endeavour as you stand surveying incredible scenery, one with the depth of Irish history, the elements and nature, not to mention standing on the same craggy, remote site as Luke Skywalker in *Star Wars*!

George Bernard Shaw describes Skellig Michael best by calling it an 'Incredible, Impossible, Mad Place.' May the Force be with you.

The Curses, Rituals and Magic of Lough Gur

Deep in County Limerick, nestled at the foot of Knockadoon Hill and Cnoc Áine, lie the mystical waters of Lough Gur. The lake itself is replenished by a series of underground springs and forms the shape of a horseshoe, which ties in nicely with the tale I am about to tell.

The land surrounding Lough Gur has history dating back more than 6000 years, and has been a place of worship and settlements dating back to the Neolithic period. Throughout the Bronze Age and Iron Age, it was home to local tribes and this continued into early Christianity and Medieval times.

As well as the discovery of Beaker Pottery, a more substantial find was discovered in the shape of what is now known as the 'Sun Shield of Lough Gur'. Straight out of the Bronze Age, this Yetholm-type piece of armory originates from the Scottish Borders and is one of only a handful that remain in the world.

The concentric circle design of the shield imitates that of a sun, which lends itself to the overall purpose and ceremonial importance of Lough Gur and the lands that touch the waters.

Within the grounds of Lough Gur stand two castles. Bourchier's Castle was built for Sir George Bourchier, son of the Earl of Bath during his time in Ireland in the late 16th century. The other is a Norman fortress known as the Black Castle. It was used during the Desmond Rebellion after the Earl of Desmond rescinded his English attire and rejoined his Irish brethren.

Ireland's Stonehenge

The Stone Circle of Grange is the largest of its kind in Ireland and is also known as *'Lios na Grainsi'* or 'Stones of the Sun'. It pre-dates much of Stonehenge and has been a place of mystical, ceremonial and sacrificial relevance for centuries.

With standing stones averaging a height of over nine feet, the circle of continuous uprights spans a diameter of just under 150 feet. There is a total of 113 standing stones and the entire structure is banked and custom made for ritualistic purpose.

Crom Dubh

The largest stone of this awe-inspiring construction is more than 13 feet high and is called Rannach Crom Dubh, or the division of *Crom Dubh* and weighs more than forty tons.

Crom Dubh is descended from the god *Crom Cruaich* and is synonymous with dark rituals, death and folklore. *Crom Cruaich* was first introduced to Ireland some time before the arrival of the Tuatha Dé Danann. Tigernmas was one of the first High Kings of Ireland and as a Milesian brought the worship of this deathly idol to Ireland, building a shrine at the top of Magh Slécht in County Cavan to win favour from his god.

King Tigernmas and most of his troops mysteriously died on Magh Slécht on the night of Samhain, now known as Halloween, as they worshipped their dark, sacrificial deity. As the centuries passed, *Crom Dubh* evolved from *Crom Cruaich* and became a worshipped figure in his own right throughout Ireland, with Lough Gur clearly no exception.

Druids and Festivals

The entire area is soaked in druidic symbolism and ritual intent. Overall, the circle is a giant astronomical calendar, in full alignment of the summer solstice. The stones themselves carry an acoustical phenomenon whereby the circle resonates with sound at certain points.

The celebration of the summer solstice continues to this day along with the festival of St, John's Night Eve on 23rd of June. The eve of the feast of Saint John the Baptist has been celebrated in Lough Gur since the formation of the early Christian fort known as Carraig Aille.

A bonfire would be ignited at sunset on the 23rd of June and kept aflame until the small hours of the following morning. Prayers and ritual blessings would take place to ensure plentiful crops and oddly to protect against drowning for the coming year.

Celebrations continued through the night including music and dance as well as games to prove prowess, strength and agility among the men. Women would be invited to jump the flames and the way in which the flames responded would supposedly reveal infidelity and misdeeds.

Áine - Queen of the Fairies

Áine is the Irish goddess of summer and prosperity, although her story is synonymous with the winter festival of Samhain.
Born of the Tuatha de Danann, Áine was said to be the daughter of The Dagda, an all-powerful god who was a father figure with immense potency and influence. He is also tied strongly to *Crom Cruaich* and *Crom Dubh*.

An eighth century text tells of Ailill Olom, King of Munster attending the festival of Samhain. He lay down to rest at what is now known as Cnoc Áine or Knockainey. When he woke, Ailill discovered all the grass had been stripped clean from the mountainside during the night.

Bewildered, the son of Eoghan Mór sought an explanation from a seer after travelling to the province of Leinster. Fearcheas mac Comáin was so fascinated by this strange turn of events, he journeyed with Ailiil back to Munster in time for Samhain once again.

As they held vigil on the Limerick mountainside, Ailill fell asleep. The King of the *Sidhe* appeared with Áine at his side. As Fearcheas crept up and murdered the Fairy King, Ailill awoke and saw the incredible vision of exquisiteness before him. Overcome with lust, he raped Áine and in rage, she tore off his ear.

The outraged goddess had reaped the ultimate revenge on her power-hungry aggressor. Under ancient Irish law, no man was fit to rule unless his body was complete. By tearing off Ailill's ear, she had forced him to rescind his crown.

Geróid Iarla and the Curse of Lough Gur

The Fairy Queen was a bewitching beauty who continued to have mortal men lusting and coveting her. Áine came down from her throne on the mountain and removed her mystical cloak to bathe in the spring waters of Lough Gur. The Earl Fitzgerald was passing by and was enchanted by her naked form. Determined to have her, he took her cloak, which left her with no choice but to do his bidding.

Their night on the banks of the lake resulted in a son who became known as The Magician. Áine returned to her land of the *Sidhe* and Geróid Iarla raised their son on the condition his inherent magical abilities were not to be encouraged in any way.

The young Geróid discovered he could shrink himself into a bottle and jump back out again. When he showed his father, the old Earl could not contain his astonishment and in his excitement, the young man jumped into the Lough, transformed into a goose and was never heard from again.

In absolute fury, the goddess came down from her throne and cursed the man responsible for the loss of her son. The Earl Fitzgerald was imprisoned beneath the lake and every seven years he rises from the waters astride his horse shod in silver.

As he rides around the lake, he looks hopefully at the horseshoes of silver on his mare's hooves. It is said that when the silver is finally worn away, Geróid Iarla can walk among mankind once again. As for Áine, she continues to watch over the sacred lake and is sometimes seen at Samhain, celebrating the magic and mystery of Lough Gur.

Innisfallen Island

Innisfallen Island lies within Lough Leane and can be reached by boat from Ross Castle. In the seventh century, Innisfallen Monastery was constructed under the eyes of St. Finian the Leper and became a place of major historical importance. Innisfallen became a seat of learning: the 1,000 -year-old hero, and legend of Ireland, Brian Boru studied here. The *Annals of Innisfallen*, a chronicle of Irish and World history was compiled on the island by a succession of monastic scribes until 1320, written in both Irish and Latin and now kept in Oxford.

The imposing remains of a large 12th century Augustinian priory and a small Roman style church are very much in evidence, and the evergreens that cover the island add to the air of foreboding and desolation on cold and bleak days. Innisfallen is a place where you can feel the weight of history and spirituality in the ground under your feet and whispered in the air around you.

Muckross Abbey

The ruins you see today, the church, cloister and courtyard, with a yew tree standing guard, are stately and well preserved, but they do not begin to tell the story of this 15th century home to the Observatine Franciscan Monks of Irrelagh and their centuries long struggle.

Donal McCarthy Mor founded Muckross Abbey in around 1448, after he allegedly had a vision telling him to found the Monastery on a rock of music. On searching the area around his home, Donal found a place on the shores of Lough Leane where mysterious music was heard with no source. This is where the foundation stone was laid. In 1589, the troops of Elizabeth I lay siege to the Abbey. However, Father Donagh O'Muirthile and his companions abandoned their residence and absconded. Before they left, the men gathered all the sacred vessels and church valuables they could carry and hid them on an island within the lake. They were captured soon after, and executed by the Queen's soldiers.

On 1st May 1698, Penal Laws were passed completely outlawing the practice of Catholicism and all Bishops and supporters were ordered to leave Ireland under threat of execution o imprisonment. Those that failed to comply or were captured were subjected to the most heinous of deaths. Hanged, ripped apart, mutilated, burned or beheaded and then weighted down and tossed into water or cremated in ovens. Those who were able to hide did so in the isolation of the Torc and Mangeton Mountains, not to return and minister openly until the late 1700s. However Muckross Abbey lay abandoned.

The site also contains a graveyard, which was the burial place of local chieftains. Three of Ireland's great poets of the 17th and 18th centuries are entombed here and the burial ground remains operational with several interments taking place each year.

Devil's Bit Mountain and The Rock of Cashel

Devil's Bit Mountain is so named, as it is believed the Devil himself took a bite from it, leaving a gap in the landscape. The bite broke his tooth, which fell from his mouth and formed the Rock of Cashel. The Rock is also known as Saint Patrick's Rock and the City of Kings. It was the seat of the kings of Munster for several hundred years, with Saint Patrick performing one of the earliest coronation ceremonies and Brian Boru was crowned here.

From the summit you can see most of Tipperary and the site has been occupied since the fourth century. There is still very much evidence of the 12th century round tower, gothic Cathedral, Cormac's Chapel and the Vicar's Hall. The Cathedral ceased use in the 1600s, as the lead was stolen by for use by alchemists.

In 1647, Earl Inchquin ransacked Cashel and the townsfolk fled to the Rock for protection, barricading themselves inside the Cathedral. Inchquin's soldiers piled turf around the outside walls and set fire to the building, leaving the 800 people inside to burn to death.

It is believed that the veil between worlds is at its thinnest on the Rock of Cashel and that many spirits and ghoulish beings haunt the land. With warriors, kings and saints laying their feet upon the ground of this ethereal place and with the unrest and bloodshed, why would you think otherwise?

The Mountain of Truth and the Fairy Castle of Donn Firinne

In Ballingarry, County Limerick, there is a mountain called Knockfierna and in that mountain is a Fairy Castle. High above anywhere else in Limerick, some 950 feet above sea level, is the top of Knockfierna or *'Knock Dhoinn Firinne'*. It translates as the Mountain of Truth, home to Donn Firinne, the Celtic God of the Dead, also known as the Chief of the Mountain and the Fairy King.

Knockfierna is full of dark history, legend and mysticism; to walk upon the craggy hillside is to take a step back in time and sate ethereal curiosity. The year 1837 saw the archaeological discovery of the Ballingarry Ogham Stone, one of only a handful found on Ireland's shores. Ogham refers to the primitive Irish text dating back to the fourth century and possibly earlier, which was carved with sharp implements into the stone as a way of recording personal information such as land ownership.

On the Strickeen lies the Lisnafeen Fairy Fort with a diameter of 100 feet, believed to be imbued with fairy magic. On the northern slope is a dolman known as 'Giant Fawha's Grave' and the Cairn or monument at the summit is believed to be the site of the ancient temple of Stuadhraicin.

But what of the fairy castle? Well let me tell you a tale - a tale of the Devil Daly...

Carroll O'Daly was a blackguard and a rogue from the Province of Connaught. He had no work and roamed from town to town without a care, a man of no respect, no fear and no consequence. He would walk through churchyards and over fairy ground at any time of day and night without protection or blessing, believing himself to be untouchable.

Finding himself in Munster, O'Daly began to head for the trading town of Kilmallock and before long found himself at the foot of Knockfierna where he met a man riding a white pony. They sauntered along in silence together and after a while, Carroll ventured to ask where the man was heading.

The man told O'Daly that they were not going the same way, as he and his white pony where heading up the hillside. Carroll asked what would take him there and the reply he received was 'The Good People'.

O'Daly said 'The Fairies?!' to which the man furiously hushed him in the event he would be sorry for his words. With that, Carroll O'Daly was wished a safe journey and the man began his ascent. Having been up to so much mischief himself, Carroll did not believe his companion and stopped to watch. The mountain was lit fully by the full moon and he could make out the silhouette of a man and a pony. His curiosity piqued, O'Daly made the decision to follow and tethered his horse to a nearby thorny tree. Cursing as he went Carroll traipsed and climbed through rugged and boggy terrain, finally stepping out into green pasture where the white pony freely grazed.

O'Daly looked around and could not see the absent rider. What he did see was a black gaping orifice in the mountainside known as the Poulnabreine or Poul Dubh, the entrance to the Fairy Castle. Carroll had heard a story as a child, of a surveyor called Ahern who decided to gauge the depth of the hole with a line, only to be drawn into the hole and never seen again.

Dismissing the story and his devilish side taking over, O'Daly decided to knock and see if the Fairy King was home. He picked up a nearby boulder with both hands and threw it with all the force he could muster into the hole. The angry sound of the rock bouncing through the mountain echoed through the night and Carroll leant in to hear it reach the bottom. Only it didn't. Before he knew what was happening a rush of air came from the opening and the very boulder he had thrown hit him square in the head so hard he was sent tumbling down the craggy hillside to the bottom of Knockfierna. The following morning, he was found alive, but severely battered and bleeding. Carroll O'Daly had his cough firmly softened and was trouble no more. The fairies were able to come out at night and dance in a ring undisturbed, the only sign of their activities being the circular beaten grass still visible in the daylight.

In later years, Knockfierna became a place of protection and refuge. A Mass Rock still plays host to religious gatherings, originally created so that the Catholics of the 1700s could take Mass in secret following the outlawing of religion during the Penal Laws under the reign of Queen Elizabeth. Famine victims sought a haven on the rugged hillside and lived in tiny hovels of stone, the foundations of which, remain today. In memory of them, a Holy Cross stands tall, protecting Knockfierna and all who fall within its shadow.

With leprechaun sightings documented as recently as 1938, and the talismans for Irish curses known as *Piseógs* found nestled in the thorns and moss, Knockfierna will always be home to 'The Good People'. My advice? Do explore the history and folklore of this wonderful place, the Mountain of Truth, but don't go knocking for entry to the fairy castle, you might never be heard of again!

Macabre Montpelier Hill – Welcome to Dublin's Hellfire Club

Montpelier Hill is an ancient mound in the County of Dublin. Its original title has long been forgotten and it got its current name from the hunting lodge built upon it. That hunting lodge became a meeting place for the Hellfire Club.

Mount Pelier Lodge

In 1725, Speaker of the House of Commons in Ireland, William Conolly erected a hunting lodge at the top of what is now known as Montpelier Hill. By building on top of an ancient burial site and using stones from the remaining cairn, the project was never going to be blessed - no one however, expected the portents of darkness to happen so soon.

With the construction almost completed, including the use of a Menhir for the mantle of the great fireplace, the roof detached and was destroyed in high winds. Locals at the time believed it to be the work of the Devil in punishment for the desecration of sacred ground.

The roof was replaced with one in an arch formation and the property was complete. The lodge was hardly used, however, and Conolly died in 1729. In around 1737, members of a secret sect leased the premises from the remaining Conolly family. In a strange twist, the land on which the lodge was built was purchased from Phillip, Duke of Wharton, and original founder of the renowned Hellfire Club. A man whose lifestyle had led him into debt and alcoholism and forced him to sell his Irish estates.

Hellfire Club

There were several Hellfire Clubs throughout Britain and Ireland. Members were of Libertine persuasion and indulged in drinking, debauchery and occult practices including ritual sacrifice. The Dublin branch of this illustrious cadre was established by Richard Parsons, the 1st Earl of Rosse and James Worsdale, a portrait artist and chancer.

Parsons was a Libertine and founder of the sacred sect of Dionysus. He was also twice elected Grandmaster of the Irish Freemasons. Worsdale on the other hand, had little to offer in pedigree and relied on his personality and own liberal approach to life to move in the most exclusive circles, his only real legacy being his portrait, 'The Hellfire Club, Dublin', hanging in the National Gallery of Ireland.

Here, as with all of the clubs, as well as identical practices and the mascot of a black cat, there were traditions to be upheld. The Hellfire gents would toast the Devil with a potent punch known as scaltheen, a heady mix of whiskey and rancid butter, whilst leaving an empty seat at the table for his arrival.

One famous tale tells of a stranger entering the club and joining the men for a game of cards. When retrieving a fallen card, a startled club member saw the guest had cloven hooves – on recognition the dark stranger vanished in flames. This story is identical to the one from the infamous Loftus Hall in Wexford, however it seems more than coincidence as the family had property on Montpelier Hill also.

There were reports of murder and animal sacrifice, including that of a black cat who was exorcised by a priest and a demon was seen fleeing. Further tales abounded of a member, Simon Luttrell who allegedly sold his soul to the Devil in order to clear his debts, to be collected in seven years. The Devil arrived at the Lodge to collect his bounty, however the resourceful Luttrell diverted the attention of his soul reaper and escaped for many more years.

During this period in the club's history, a horrendous fire took hold during a meeting and several lives were lost. The exact cause of the fire is unknown, yet claims have been made of everything from a footman accidentally spilling a flammable drink to the deliberate act of the members due to a non-renewal of lease. Either way, the club moved premises to the Steward's House some short distance down the hill. Now the remains of the Lodge stand in ruins, but not abandoned, at least not by the living.

The screams of a woman being bowled to her death in a burning barrel echo over the hill, a smell of brimstone fills the air and invisible hands grabbing at throats to tear off jewellery are just some of the claims of paranormal activity at the top of Montpelier Hill.

Steward's House

Built in around 1765, the property became a welcome replacement for the burned-out lodge as a meeting place for the Club where the depraved practices continued until the Hellfire club was extinguished with the demise of notorious member and revivalist of the same, Thomas "Buck" Whaley.

In the late 1960s, workers began repairs and renovations to the Steward's House and witnessed many apparitions including that of a man in black believed to be the priest who exorcised the cat at the Hellfire Club at Mount Pelier Lodge.

Further sightings were made of nuns alleged to have participated in black masses on the hill and a black cat with glowing red eyes.

Other activities include hearing the sounds of bells ringing and poltergeist activity. In 1971 a plumber, carrying out work, unearthed a grave containing the remains of a child or small human, and thought to be a ritual sacrifice of the brethren of the Hellfire Club.

Massy's Estate

In the late 19th century, the Massy family of Limerick took ownership of Killakee House and surrounding land on Montpelier Hill. In a cruel twist reminiscent of those involved with the Hellfire Club, the party loving Baron Hugh Massy who inherited the property from his family was declared bankrupt, becoming known as the Penniless Peer. The house itself was destroyed upon repossession.

With the exception of the Steward's House, which is privately owned, the area on Montpelier Hill including the Hellfire Club site and remaining cairn form Lord Massy's Estate, open to the public.

The subject of many paranormal investigations, the Lodge, Steward's House and surrounding Massy woods remain a place of mystery with little documented evidence to verify many of the stories and alleged events, largely due to the isolation and secrecy of the Hellfire Club.

That said, when you build a lodge by desecrating a sacred burial site, then invite members of the one of the darkest and debauched societies in history to carry out their Devil Worship in that location, macabre occurrences are guaranteed.

So look for your proof as needs be, although perhaps searching for protection from the Devil would be more prudent – and if you smell brimstone, run, before you become a permanent member of the Hellfire Club.

HAUNTINGS, DARK HISTORY AND DESPAIR

Massacre at the Fortress of Gold

On the Dingle Peninsula lies the Viking settlement of Smerwick Harbour. On it was built the settlement of Dún an Óir, also known as 'Fort del Oro' or 'The Fortress of Gold'. In the latter 16th century explorers returning from the Arctic hit a reef and sank their ship with a cargo hold full of black gold. This was later to be revealed as Fool's Gold and the worthless load was said to be utilised as building blocks for the fort.

In 1579, James Maurice Fitzgerald initiated the Second Desmond Rebellion against the English and those who sided with them. He took position with his men at Smerwick and was slain within the month. Undeterred, the rebellion continued, and Pope Gregory XIII sent Papal troops in September of 1580, led by Sebastian di San Giuseppe to give aid to Fitzgerald's army.

Although only numbering around 600 in total, thanks to the arms and money brought over from Europe, the men of Desmond were able to hold off the English who were in a holding pattern until the arrival of Admiral Winter and the Lord Deputy of Ireland, Arthur Grey, together with a few thousand naval personnel.

Trapped by the ships blockade in the bay, Grey's men advancing and the daunting Mount Bandon behind them, Giuseppe had no choice but to order his men to retreat to Dún an Óir. They battled on for three days as the English laid siege to the fortress, however they were left with no alternative but to surrender without condition.

In November of 1580, overseen by Sir Walter Raleigh, the Rebellion and Papal Troops were gathered, and the officers led away. The remaining 600 or so men were taken to a field now known as 'Gort a Gherradh' or 'The Field of Cutting' for execution. Every last man was put to his knees and beheaded.

The heads were buried together in a field and the bodies thrown without ceremony into the sea. It is said these soldiers were the lucky ones as the officers were to suffer a worse fate. The higher-ranking men were told to immediately denounce their Catholic faith in order to receive a life sentence. The captives' refusal to do so led to their limbs being fractured multiple times, after which they were left in agony for a day before being dragged out and hanged.

In later years, some would say the dead had their revenge, as although only acting on instruction, Raleigh was charged with atrocities pertaining to the events at Dún an Óir as well as the Main Plot against James I, which led to his own execution.

Centuries later the fort is ruins, victim of an unforgiving sea and the field in which the heads of the soldiers are buried has been named '*Gort na gCeann*'. A sculpture has been placed here to commemorate the dead of the Second Desmond Rebellion, but this is not enough to let their spirits rest in peace.

The harsh erosion of the Atlantic coast is said to have brought skulls and skeletons forth from their burial site and on the anniversary of the massacre, the tormented souls call out. Many have heard voices crying out in Spanish, the agonising sounds of fear and suffering not needing translation and on the wind, the horrific stench of rotting flesh is carried out to sea. If you stand on Smerwick Harbour, remember you stand on centuries old violent history and bloodshed. If you are standing there in November, the men of the Second Desmond Rebellion will not let you forget it.

Loftus Hall – Ireland's Most Haunted House

Loftus Hall is known as Ireland's most haunted house, and with good reason. Overlooking acres of a desolate and harsh landscape on the Hook Peninsula, County Wexford, this three-storey mansion owned by Aiden Quigley has been the subject of several paranormal investigations, including many by paranormal investigative team, Irish Ghost Hunters.

Loftus Hall is a place so notoriously dark and foreboding, the Devil himself made it his home for a while.

History

There has been a residence on the site since the Redmond family built their home on lands they acquired on the Hook Peninsula. In 1350 at the height of The Black Death, they erected their formal home and estate, which would remain in their possession until the mid-17th century.

During the height of the Cromwellian invasion, head of the family Alexander Redmond defended his home time and again from the English onslaught and eventually retained his property under agreement until his death. At this point, the remaining Redmond family were evicted under Cromwellian confiscations.

The Loftus family were English and were located in the surrounding area. They were formally granted ownership of the estate by the reinstated King Charles II, with son Henry Loftus taking up official residence in 1666, a year that may well have been a portent of events to come. The Redmond family, feeling hard done by disputed ownership through the courts, however their efforts failed - an outcome they would have been thankful for in the long run no doubt!

In 1917 Loftus Hall was purchased by a religious order and adapted into a convent and school for girls wishing to take Holy Vows. It continued under religious ownership until Michael Deveraux purchased it in 1983. Mr. Deveraux converted the imposing historical building into a hotel and spent much effort and money to create the Loftus Hall Hotel. It would appear that the house was in some way cursed to failure, as the hotel was forced to close just a few short years later. Loftus Hall remained under ownership of the Deveraux family until 2011, at which point it was purchased as an abandoned building by the current proprietor Aidan Quigley.

The Stranger, the Card Game, Anne Tottenham and the Devil

While under the ownership of the Loftus family, Charles Tottenham, his second wife and daughter from his first marriage, Anne, arrived at Loftus Hall. They were there to mind the property as the proprietors were away on business in 1766.

During their occupation, an unusually heavy storm covered the Hook Peninsula in fog and an unfamiliar ship set anchor. A stranger arrived at Loftus Hall seeking refuge from the tempest and was welcomed into the home.

The charismatic young man soon charmed his way into the affections of Anne Tottenham and the couple began relations under the roof of Loftus Hall.

One night the family were sat around the table playing cards with the mysterious visitor dealing. As Anne seemed to only have been dealt two cards as opposed to the usual three, she glanced to the floor to see a third one lying beneath the table.

Assuming she had dropped it, Anne stooped down to retrieve the fallen card. At this point, she cried out in horror, as she saw that the man she had given her heart to had cloven hooves for feet.

Upon being discovered, the creature shot skyward, smashing a hole through the roof of Loftus Hall. Anne Tottenham became crazed with grief over her lost love and was an embarrassment to her family. She was locked out of sight in the Tapestry Room, where she sat hunched, not taking any sustenance -just staring out of the window pining and hoping for the return of the ship to Dunmore East until she died.

Exorcism

It was believed that the presence of the Dark Lord lingered, and poltergeist activity became rife in the house, escalating to such a point that the Protestant clergy were powerless to abate it. In desperation the Loftus family called upon Father Thomas Broaders, a Catholic priest residing on the townland also known as Loftus Hall. He performed an exorcism and appeared to banish the demons within.

Broaders rose to the position of Parish Priest and remained as Canon until his death in 1773. He is buried in the old Horetown Cemetery and his gravestone reads:

"Here lies the body of Thomas Broaders,
Who did good and prayed for all.
And banished the Devil from Loftus Hall."

Hauntings

For all his good work, the priest had failed to drive the supernatural from Loftus Hall. The spectre of a lady believed to be the tormented Anne Tottenham has been seen over the years, in the Tapestry room and walking down the grand staircase.

As recently as 2014 a tourist taking a photograph was astounded to discover what appeared to be the ghostly image of a woman appearing in the window. Disembodied children's voices, phantom cries and the sound of ghostly horses have all fallen on terrified ears. Sudden temperature drops, feelings of foreboding and flickering lights have all been witnessed.

Lucifer and Loftus Hall

If the account of the Devil reminds you of another tale you may have heard, it should. An identical story was told of a card game being held at the notorious Hellfire Club of Dublin on Montpelier Hill, where a stranger with cloven hooves for feet sat at the table. As well as the Hellfire Club, Montpelier Hill was the site of a hunting lodge known as Dolly Mount. This lodge was owned by Henry Loftus.

The question must be asked, with Henry Loftus taking residence in 1666 and the second visit by a cloven hooved stranger to the Hellfire Club on the very land in Dublin previously owned by the Loftus family, was Anne Tottenham an unfortunate victim in the wrong place at the wrong time? What is the meaning of the Loftus association with signs of the Devil and was a pact made with Lucifer for the Redmond Estate? We will never know for sure, however recent years marked the 666th anniversary of the founding of the Mansion House known as Loftus Hall – will Satan return again and will you dare to be there if he does?

Through the Gates of Hell - Dare you enter Haunted Wicklow Gaol?

Situated in Ireland's Ancient East, the County town of Wicklow is shadowed by the imposing and sinister Wicklow Gaol. For more than three hundred years, prisoners have been subjected to torture and hardship and the three-storey building, with sprawling foundations and walls of granite has witnessed some of Ireland's must oppressive and historical events.

History of Wicklow Gaol

Since 1702, there has been a prison on the site at Kilmartin Hill. The existing buildings were constructed over the remnants of the first gaol and were gradually expanded over the 18th and 19th centuries. The Rebellion of 1798 brought ongoing notoriety to the prison as freedom fighters were jailed before trial and exile or execution. This pattern continued through the Famine, Easter Rising of 1916 and the Irish Civil War.

In the mid-19th century, overcrowding at Wicklow Gaol brought expansion, as the authorities feared the granite walls themselves would collapse under the pressure. Britain was forced to bring about changes due to European Prison Reform, and that included the gaols of Ireland and as a result; facilities now included classrooms, workrooms and proper medical quarters. The prison was downsized in 1877 and renamed a 'Bridewell', which was a remand prison for those awaiting trial and sentencing for petty crimes.

In later years, Wicklow Gaol had lain dormant for some time; however the Irish Civil War of 1922-23 brought the prison back into use for political prisoners, primarily members of the Irish Republican Brotherhood and Sinn Féin, including Erskine Childers, notable Irish Nationalist and gun smuggler. The early 20th century also brought in a change of use to an army barracks. It became home to the Cheshire regiment, which in a strange twist of fate, was founded 30 years previously by none other than Hugh Childers, cousin of one of Wicklow Gaol's most famous prisoners. Finally, in 1924 the Gates of Hell closed on the prison as it fell into disuse and disrepair, until it was respectfully restored and opened to the public.

Crimes, Punishment and Exile

The prison was used for years for general convictions; however, the 1798 rebellion saw its use change to include the incarceration of political prisoners. Many inmates, from those rebelling against the Crown to petty thieves were taken from Wicklow Gaol to the convict ships and exiled to distant lands such as Australia. A replica of the deck of the convict ship HMS Hercules has been built inside the gaol. There was no segregation within the prison as such, and people who had stolen to provide food for their families in times of hardship found themselves sharing with the mentally ill, murderers and political prisoners.

Those who were exiled may have deemed themselves lucky, as the torture and methods of execution, poor conditions and suffering were unpleasant and unending. Prison reforms introduced rehabilitation through education, although attempts at segregation, silence and torture were the preferred methods of atonement.

Torture devices included the everlasting staircase, a treadmill of sorts designed for maximum fatigue, breaking of spirit and isolation and a shot drill, a metal ball that was required to be held for periods of time suited to the prison guard, or else loss of rations would be enforced. Flogging was by far the most favoured form of punishment, especially due to increased numbers of local workers being imprisoned for drunk and disorderly conduct.

When it came to execution, in the early 18th century, prisoners would be hanged from the gallows arm jutting out of the prison walls. After death, the head would be severed from the body, which would be buried. The head was then scavenged and eaten by the gaol's 'pet' hawk. Other bodies would be unceremoniously dumped at sea, until the problem became enough for local fishermen to threaten to stop fishing due to pollution.

Disease, Death and Dire Conditions

Overcrowding was a consistently major problem and expansion just couldn't keep up with demand, peaking at an inmate population of almost 800 being housed in just 77 cells. As a result, the spread of disease was rife and death wasn't far behind. Often if a prisoner died of an infection they were left in the crowded cell, the rotting and diseased corpse bringing about the hideous deaths of those within the four walls, prison guards or 'turnkeys' just looking on, afraid to enter for fear of becoming a victim themselves.

The Great Famine of 1845-1852 brought around a very different kind of problem. Upstanding citizens would commit crime in order to be incarcerated in Wicklow Gaol, as prison reforms guaranteed them shelter and regular meals – life staples they could not get on the outside. There were no asylums or care facilities for the mentally ill in Wicklow, so the insane were mixed in with the general population. The women prisoners would be responsible for the welfare of these inmates.

Attempts were made to 'employ' prisoners for local work such as making nets for fishermen, however this practice stopped due to a growing fear of authorities that these items would be used in an attempt to escape.

Infamous Inmates

Some of Ireland's most famous rebel sons and at least one daughter were incarcerated for their attempts to bring about political change and create a Free State. This included Billy Byrne, mounter of several ambush attacks during the 1798 rebellion who was tried and then hanged at Gallows' Lane.

James 'Napper' Tandy worked long and hard for political change, however after a short imprisonment he was exiled to France despite being convicted of treason. It is believed Napoleon may have exerted some influence, hence his designated place of exile.

Erskine Childers was a London born author and avid sailor. A firm believer in Ireland as a free nation, Childer's used his yacht the *Asgard* to smuggle guns into the east coast of Ireland. He was arrested after being found in possession of a gun, a gift from Michael Collins. Childers was convicted and executed by firing squad on 24th of November 1922.

Hauntings

Wicklow Gaol has been the subject of paranormal activity for centuries and has attracted worldwide interest from paranormal investigators. Those brave enough to join the Paranormal Researchers Ireland team for a lockdown will find themselves at the centre of a myriad of supernatural experiences.

At least one medium has entered Wicklow Gaol and claimed to have made contact with Erskine Childers, however there have been many witnesses to other phenomena. A young child is regularly seen in the former school room and can also be heard. Other 'inmates' of the spectral variety are seen shimmering in and out of cells and along walkways.

On the replica of the Hercules deck, visitors are overcome with a sense of foreboding and eerie mists circle unsuspecting visitors. Certain cells have been the epicentre of extraordinary paranormal occurrences including smells from the stagnant to the sublime, female apparitions in black floating and sounds to terrify the hardiest of souls. A ghostly prisoner can be seen on the walkway, hands behind his back and the eerie sounds of long gone children fill the ancient prison.

Cork City Gaol

Built to replace the old, overcrowded prison, Cork City Gaol was opened to prisoners in 1824. An imposing gothic style citadel just two kilometers from the very heart of Cork City, the prison remained home to both male and female convicts over the course of almost one hundred years. After been an all-women's gaol from 1878, the final inmates were male Republicans who fought against the Anglo-Irish treaty during the Irish Civil War of 1922-1923.

In August of 1923, the prison closed its entrance gates to the incarcerated for the last time. The question however, is did everyone leave? Now a heritage centre, visitors often report the sound of the shuffling feet of inmates in the West Wing and voices are heard throughout the gaol. When the centre first opened in 1993, workers heard the sound of a child saying "Daddy". Their investigations led to them to be confronted by the spectral image of a lady in a green shawl.

The prison is valued not only as a place of heritage, but for its paranormal reputation and for years has played host to the Annual Irish Ghost Convention, which takes place each October. Open to visitors all year round, you can step through the gates and into the gaol, alert for the residual sights and sounds of long ago. If you are brave enough you can always take the night tour, however be warned that the sound of scuffing shoes behind you and the whisper in your ear may not be from a fellow tourist!

St. Finbarr's Hospital, Cork City

A working hospital today, St Finbarr's started life in 1840 as the Cork Union Workhouse. Some were held here against their will and some used it as a place of refuge because they simply had nowhere else to go. At the time of the Great Famine from 1845-1852 the building was pushed beyond its limits and over 2,000 citizens were housed in sheds and outbuildings. The disease and horror of destitution was never more real and deadly.

The facility also became home to the Cork Fever Hospital. Diphtheria, Typhoid and Tuberculosis were rife, and people were dying in the hundreds weekly, their disease-ridden bodies carted away via the passageways running beneath the buildings. At the start of the twentieth century, the premises became the County Home for the Infirm and District Hospital.

In truth, the buildings became a place to put those deemed to be a nuisance to society and became home to the elderly, unmarried mothers and their children as well as the criminally insane and those in need of psychiatric care. Now a hospital with specialist units, over many years the same ghost has been seen and spoken of by patients and staff alike.

The ghost of a nun, believed to be from the 1940s, is seen on the upper floors of the hospital, which always housed the medical cases. She walks around the wards and corridors, as if doing her rounds and checking on her charges, believed to speak to children as she goes. A place of tragedy and despair, it would be hard to imagine how there wouldn't be remnants of the past remaining.

Carr's Hill Cemetery

The worst point of the famine was in the winter of 1846/47 and it became known as 'Black 47'. It was the worst in living memory and those living in rural communities fled to the city believing they would find refuge and food. This influx brought the already crippled city to its knees and many were left to die in the streets. Cemeteries inside the city boundaries were overflowing so a local landowner saw an opportunity to turn a profit from misery by releasing some of his land just outside of Cork city.

Known as Carr's Hole, with at least 5,000 bodies interred, the mass graves contained so many coffins the ones at the top of the plots were barely covered with earth and the putrid stench of decaying flesh filled the air. While there have been no sightings documented, Carr's Hill cemetery as with all famine cemeteries are whispered about locally as a place where the dead cannot rest.

Unfortunately, tragedy doesn't finish there, as the graveyard continued to be used as a Pauper's burial site until the 1950s. Dying in poverty and disease, these victims were buried like animals in unconsecrated ground, no dignity and no grave markings - a person would be hard pressed to not sense something in this place. Be careful not to step upon the Hungry Grass covering the dead however, you don't want to become a victim too.

Our Lady's Hospital and St Kevin's Asylum, Cork

Our Lady's hospital, also known as Eglinton Asylum, was originally built to accommodate 500 patients. However, demand was such it was extended further and finally, in 1852, admissions began into the 1000 feet long gothic monstrosity. Our Lady's Hospital continually failed to meet with demand and so in 1893 St Kevin's was built as an annex, linked by an extensive passageway, the majority of which was underground.

Conditions were atrocious and reports spanning from 1934 to 1940 recorded mattresses on floors, unsanitary living conditions, no basic amenities and inmates being subjected to filth and squalor, describing the situation as a 'Chapter of Horrors.' Due to its proximity to the River Lee, many patient deaths were as a result of drowning. St Kevin's itself remained a mental institution until closure in 2002.

It became abandoned, although some parts were being renovated into living accommodation. Known in paranormal circles worldwide, St Kevin's has earned itself the reputation of being the creepiest place in Cork. Those who have ventured into the dark, oppressive corridors and rooms of this historical atrocity describe it as intense and unwelcoming.

There is a constant feeling of someone over your shoulder and the sounds of heels clicking on the derelict floor. Even the most seasoned of ghost hunters have said it is impossible to stay more than a couple of hours before being overcome with the thick, heavy air of evil in the place. Sadly, the site burned down as a result of arson, and it lies an empty shell. One thing is for sure-some of the old residents remain and it is not a place for the faint hearted.

Ross Castle, Killarney

On Ross Island, on the shores of Lough Leane (The Lake of Learning), stands the distinguished Ross Castle. Built in the late 15th Century, it's positioning and structure made the castle very effective for defence throughout its long and varied history.

Originally built by O'Donoghue Mór, during the Desmond wars it was handed to the McCarty Mórs who successfully defended against Oliver Cromwell's army until 1652. Although the army numbered thousands of soldiers and horses, Ross Castle was proving virtually impenetrable, so they chose to take the fortress by boat. There was believed to be an old Irish prophecy that Ross Castle would only succumb to invasion when a ship swam upon the lake. Could this prophecy have been instrumental in the surrender of the McCarty Mór Clan?

Foretold or by advanced military tactics, Ross Castle was taken by force and remained under English control. It was handed to loyalist Sir Valentine Browne and remained home to the Browne family until the 18th century. From here, it was a military barracks, until decommissioning in 1825. Now open to the public, for 150 years it was unused - but not abandoned.

There was one keeper lingering, the original owner O'Donoghue. He is thought to have lain at the bottom of Lough Leane all this time, watching Ross Castle. On the 1st of May, every seven years he mounts his horse and rides the shores of the Lake. If you seem him, you are said to be assured of good fortune for the rest of your life.

The Lake Hotel, Killarney

Standing on Lough Leane, overlooking Ross Castle, The Lake Hotel was built in 1820 and still holds many of its original features. Believed to have played host to Queen Victoria during her visit to these shores, it has always been family owned and this sense of homeliness has meant some guests are permanent.

The founder of Muckross Abbey, Donal McCarthy Mór apparently likes to keep watch on the Castle and Abbey from the comfort of the Hotel. Known locally as 'Dan the Feathers', McCarthy was a ruthless warrior and was said to have made a bed from the feathers of the Queen's troops that he killed in battle. It was believed to have survived until the 19th century in the Lake Hotel itself, and Dan has been seen in the hotel's Devil's Punchbowl Bar looking out over Lough Leane.

There is also supposed to be the spirit of a young girl from the 1800s who wanders the corridors, leaving a chill in the air and a sense of serenity with those who encounter her. A psychic has apparently tried to make contact, however as the girl was speaking an old local dialect she could not be understood, so her identity and reasons for remaining are unknown.

Glin Castle, Glin, Limerick

Standing on the banks of the River Shannon Estuary is Glin Castle, over 700 years old and home to the Fitzgerald family and the Knights of Glin. The 29th and last Knight of Glin, Desmond Fitzgerald died in September 2011 and the title was laid to rest with him.

The Castle has been the subject of reported hauntings and poltergeist activity over a number of years. Many of the hauntings are thought to be the souls of those who fell during the many battles on the site and still roam the 500-acre estate. On the third floor of the Castle, witnessed poltergeist activity has included lights flicking on and off and doors rapidly opening and closing. A frayed rope was found hanging from a ceiling where a worker was killed some years previously when the rope on his safety harness snapped. A builder called Henry appears on the staircase just to pass the time and the 20th Knight of Glin himself can be found sitting in his favourite chair.

St Katherine's Abbey Ruins, Shanagolden, Limerick

Saint Katherine's Augustinian Abbey was one of the first nunneries in Ireland, founded in 1298. It is now just ruins, with the remains of the Abbey Church and Refectory still evident. It is believed that the last Abbess prior to the Abbey's dissolution in 1541 practiced witchcraft in a room south of the Church, which became known as The Black Hag's Cell.

The ruins themselves are haunted by the Countess of Desmond. The Earl and Countess were fleeing an assault and during their escape the Countess was wounded by an arrow. Believing her to be dead, her husband buried his wife in haste beneath the altar at St Katherine's. The Countess regained consciousness only to find herself buried alive. A shadowy figure is seen among the ruins and the Countess's screams still ring out in the night as she cries for her husband to realise his mistake.

Castle Matrix, Rathkeale, Limerick

Castle Matrix is situated about a mile from the centre of town. Built by the Fitzgerald Dynasty in 1420 for the seventh Earl of Desmond, the name itself is believed to derive from 'Madres', the triple-mother goddesses of the Pagan Celts. In 1487, James, Ninth Earl of Desmond who was not a popular master among his servants, owned the Castle. On the 7th of December his servants decided they would be rid of the Earl and together they brutally murdered him.

Upon hearing this, James's brother Maurice avenged his death by executing every single servant they had. Although Castle Matrix has been a family home for many years, James still haunts the castle to this day. If you can find Castle Matrix and dare to knock on the door, you may be lucky enough that a member of the O'Driscoll family will show you around!

The Dark History and Hauntings Cobh

Originally, the assembly point for the Napoleonic fleets, Cobh nestles in the shadow of the majestic St. Colman's Cathedral, which is said to have a phantom Black Hound guarding its foundations. Cobh looks out over Cork Harbour and Haulbowline and Spike Islands, into the Atlantic Ocean. It was named Queenstown in 1850 after a state visit from Queen Victoria and Prince Albert and reverted back to Cobh in 1920. With such a history and so many paranormal occurrences, it seems only right to take a closer look at some of the events, sights and claims taking place over the past hundred years.

RMS Titanic

On Thursday 11th of April 1912, the RMS Titanic loomed over the Port of Queenstown, where it had docked to board more travellers and the mail. 123 Irish passengers boarded boats on the wooden pier that remains to this day and were rowed out to the colossal ship, dreams of a new life in America eclipsed by the excitement of the vastness of the Ocean Liner waiting for them. Cheered on by the townspeople on the promenade and pier, Titanic raised anchor for the final time and at 1.30pm headed west for New York, no idea of the horror that was to befall her and her 2,228 crew and passengers just four days later, never to see land again. Of the passengers who boarded in Queenstown, only 44 survived.

To stand by the wooden pier, where those travellers stood, knowing it was the last time 79 of them would ever stand on dry land is eerie even on the brightest day and a shiver can be felt as you imagine the excitement of the immigrants turning to fear and terror in the freezing dark waters of the Atlantic.

In the heritage centre, built onto the Victorian railway line, which would have brought many of the passengers into Cobh, poltergeist activity has been rife, with workmen's' tools being scattered and a crystal in the main heritage shop being taken from a shelf in the night and placed carefully in the centre of the shop floor.

On the pier behind the heritage centre the spirit of a young woman in a red cape has been seen floating through the gates, looking expectantly out to sea.

Commodore Hotel

Ireland's first custom built hotel opened for business in 1854 and its focus was to attract the many passengers embarking on voyages including the Titanic. At the time of the sinking of the Lusitania by German U Boat, the hotel was under German ownership. Otto

Humbert and his family were forced to hide in the cellars as a crowd gathered and demanded the hotel be burned to the ground. Instead, the hotel was converted into a hospital and makeshift morgue for the hundreds of victims.

While locals feel there must be some residual energy left from the fear and torment of the poor passengers, the haunting most reported is that of a crying baby on the upper floors of the hotel, where the body of an infant was alleged to have been found abandoned in one of the rooms.

Spike Island

Spike Island lies just off the coast of Cobh and is reached by ferry; the island spans more than 100 acres and has a history going back to the seventh century. Originally a monastic community, its location on the edge of Cork Harbour meant it was of strategic significance for everyone from smugglers to the French, British and Irish militaries.

In 1779, Spike Island became a fort for British forces, with casements built so that guns were facing into the harbour. As time progressed, the fort became a prison and convict-holding site for those unfortunates being shipped out to penal colonies. During the Irish War of Independence IRA prisoners were held until 1921 and it became known as Ireland's Alcatraz.

The island was maintained as both a jail and military base until the latter 20th century when it became a Youth Correctional Facility. After a riot that lead to the remaining island civilians, Gardaí and prison officers being virtual prisoners themselves, the facility was wound down.

Spike Island is now a tourist attraction, much the same as Alcatraz and is not without its own ghosts. A spectre known as the White Woman haunts the island and the perimeter walls are guarded by a phantom soldier staring through black hollows where his eyes once were.

If tragedy and despair are triggers for hauntings, then I cannot think of a more obvious place to find them. To the naked eye, Cobh appears to have been lost in time, as Victorian now as it ever was, with brightly coloured houses, original hotel façade, promenade and bandstand. This port town however has not been lost in time continuing to be a port of call for the world's largest cruise ships where all the passengers take in the historic surroundings and then sail off into the Atlantic Ocean, bound for a new port -well almost all......of course some never leave.

Ghosts of RMS Lusitania and the Port Of Cobh

A picturesque town with strong regal connections, it is hard to imagine that Cobh is synonymous with two of the biggest passenger liner tragedies of all time, just three years apart - RMS Titanic and *RMS Lusitania*.

On the 7th of May 2015, Cobh made itself ready to mark the 100th anniversary of the First World War tragedy, the sinking of the *RMS Lusitania*. What part did the former Queenstown play in the disaster and why do some of the victims of the sinking refuse to leave?

Construction and Use of the Lusitania

Built in Scotland, the Lusitania was largely funded by the Admiralty, as Europe was in a state of unrest and conflict was believed imminent. By contributing to the cost and overseeing the construction, the Navy would be able to call on the 787 feet liner in the event of war, while in the meantime, she was one of Cunard's front running cruise vessels setting records for speed.

The Lusitania had made 201 successful transatlantic voyages as a passenger ship since 1907. Once war broke out, the cruiser was also used to ship weapons to Britain with travellers knowing little or anything about the additional military cargo stored a few decks beneath their feet.

The Cunard liner was painted camouflage grey as war approached but continued to be used as a passenger vessel.

The Fateful Crossing

On the 1st of May 1915, *RMS Lusitania* set sail from New York for Liverpool on her 202nd voyage with 1,962 passengers and crew on board.

By now the cruise ship had been transformed to her initial glory from the camouflage grey, however she was not bearing flags in marked out war zones, contravening Cruiser Rules dictated by the First World War. These rules were set to safeguard passengers in the event of capture or attack and prevent any misidentification by the enemy.

The ship set sail from Pier 54 in New York despite the following statement from the German Embassy being printed in dozens of American newspapers:

"Notice!
Travellers intending to embark on the Atlantic voyage are reminded that a state of war exists between Germany and her allies and Great Britain and her allies; that the zone of war includes the waters adjacent to the British Isles; that, in accordance with formal notice given by the Imperial German Government, vessels flying the flag of Great Britain, or any of her allies, are liable to destruction in those waters and that travellers sailing in the war zone on the ships of Great Britain or her allies do so at their own risk.
Imperial German Embassy
Washington, D.C., April 22, 1915."

Although the ship's manifest openly documented munitions in the cargo hold, the extent of undocumented firepower has never been fully disclosed and undoubtedly contributed to the Lusitania's demise.

Kinsale and The Torpedo

As *RMS Lusitania* approached the south coast of Ireland, a German U Boat crossed her path and due to the nature of her cargo, prior warnings and without the relevant flags, the captain of the U-20 give an order to fire. The Lusitania sustained a direct hit, which in turn caused further explosions within the hull, most likely due to the extent of ammunition and artillery on board.

Due to the lack of lifeboats being launched, poor execution of evacuation and the way in which she tilted and descended, the Lusitania sank to the bottom of the sea, just 11 miles from Kinsale, County Cork in just 20 minutes.

The sinking of the Lusitania, both in speed and manner was eerily reminiscent of RMS Titanic, just three years earlier. Despite rescue efforts from localised fishing vessels, 1,201 souls were lost.

Aftershock

Some of the deceased were brought to Kinsale by rescue boats and interred at St Multose Church, while it was also in Kinsale that the local Coroner launched an official enquiry the following day.

The majority of the bodies however, were either brought to or washed up in Cobh, (Queenstown as it was known at the time) along with the few survivors. In the Old Church Cemetery, just on the outskirts of Cobh, almost 200 of the victims of the tragedy are buried in mass and individual graves. Of course, many more were never recovered at all.

In a sickening coincidence, Ireland's first custom built hotel, The Commodore opened for business in 1854 and its focus was to attract the many passengers embarking on voyages including the Titanic and Lusitania. At the time of the sinking of the Lusitania by a German U Boat, the hotel was under German ownership. Otto Humbert and his family were forced to hide in the cellars as a crowd gathered and demanded the hotel be burned to the ground. The hotel itself was then converted into a hospital and makeshift morgue for the victims.

Hauntings

While locals feel there must be some residual energy left from the fear and torment of the poor passengers within Cobh and particularly The Commodore Hotel, the haunting most reported is one witnessed on more than one occasion from a diverse section of the community, including the White Witch of Cobh and a Graves Inspector.

This supernatural event is none other than the chilling sound of a mass funeral procession for the victims of the Lusitania which had taken place on the 10th of May 1915. The White Witch herself claims to have 'seen' it, however most accounts refer to many low murmuring voices and the sound of footsteps approaching the cemetery wall. Some have in fact assumed a current funeral was approaching and have looked up to see nothing but an empty road. With so much maritime tragedy at its heart, it is no wonder that as well as the broken bodies of the victims of the *RMS Lusitania* remaining in Cobh, the despairing spirits also remain.

Haunted Pubs of Dublin

John Kavanagh 'The Gravediggers' Pub, 1 Prospect Square, Glasnevin, Dublin 9

Located beside the famous Glasnevin Cemetery, Kavanagh's is where body snatchers would wind down after a hard night of stealing corpses and during the day thirsty gravediggers would throw a handful of earth at the pub wall in order to scare up a pint! An elderly gentleman dressed in a dated tweed suit sits at the bar sipping a pint and when he has finished, simply fades away.

Davy Byrne's Pub, 21 Duke Street, Dublin 2

This public house has been around for more than 125 years, with the upstairs room being used for Republican meetings and frequented by Michael Collins himself. It is however, most famous for its associations with James Joyce and it is immortalised in the pages of Ulysses. James Joyce seemed to enjoy Davy Byrne's so much that he never left, his reflection regularly seen in the bar mirrors.

Bull And Castle, 5-7 Lord Edward Street, Dublin 8

James Clarence Mangan was a famous Irish poet and patriot born in 1803 on what is now the site of the Bull and Castle public house. As a poet he was greatly admired by the likes of Yeats and Joyce, however as a man he was a solitary figure, suffering with depression and addiction. He dressed bizarrely in a long cloak, green spectacles and a blond wig. Patrons have been sat in the bar, merry and playful, when an icy chill sweeps over the entire premises and the mood darkens and all become melancholy, a sure sign that James Mangan is home for a visit.

The Brazen Head, 20 Lower Bridge Street, Dublin 8

Dating back to 1198, the Brazen Head has the official title of Ireland's oldest public house. Clientele have included James Joyce, Jonathan Swift and freedom fighters Wolfe Tone, Michael Collins and Daniel O'Connell. One leading revolutionary of the 1803 uprising was

Robert Emmet and he held his meetings in the Brazen Head. Captured and put on trial, Emmet was about to be cleared as the trial unravelled, until his own lawyer turned against him. The 25-year-old was found guilty of treason and hanged, drawn and quartered. Death did not stop Robert Emmet's duty of care however and he remains in the Brazen Head keeping watch for the enemy.

Madigan's Bar, Connolly Station, Amiens Street, Dublin 1

Busy commuter station Connolly is in the heart of Dublin and Madigan's Bar is right on the concourse. There have been so many reports of ghosts and poltergeist activity in and around Connolly Station and Madigan's Bar that in 2011 Irish Ghost Hunters undertook an investigation to see what was happening. So if you feel a tug at your briefcase as you sip your pint, don't assume there's a thief behind it - not a living one anyway.

Brogans, 75 Dame Street, Dublin 1

Formally known as Leonards, this centuries old establishment stands beside the Olympia Theatre. It has been featured in the 1969 book, 'Irish Pubs of Character' and counted Michael Collins among its regular patrons. It is little surprise given its proximity to the haunted Olympia, that there have been reports of eerie footsteps and poltergeist activity including a door being smashed. The most interesting thing about Brogans however, is the belief that there is, or certainly was, a secret passageway running from the pub, underneath Dame Street and straight into Dublin Castle!

The Portobello, 33 South Richmond Street, Dublin 2

Situated on the banks of the Grand Canal, this pub by the bridge is the site of the spectre of a drunken lock keeper who drowned himself in the canal. His drinking habits caused the deaths of the passengers in a horse drawn carriage in the mid-19th century and he could not live with the deaths and being fired. His spirit is a bitter and vengeful one however, as the phenomenon associated with the lock keeper is a light so searing and powerful, it creates confusion and dizziness, causing some to fall into the icy canal.

The Lord Edward Pub, 23 Werburgh Street, Christchurch Place, Dublin 8

Lord Edward Fitzgerald was against the Crown and he played a vital role in the planning of the rebellion at the beginning of the 19th century. Fitzgerald did not get to see the rebellion however, as he was discovered hiding in nearby Thomas Street and attempts were made to arrest Edward for treason. He fought against his captors and was severely wounded; however, he was still taken to Newgate Gaol where he later died of his wounds. He is buried in St. Werburgh's Church, right across from the entrance to his namesake pub. Lord Edward's shade is said to roam the bar, defending those within.

Doyles Pub, 160 Doyles Corner, North Circular Road, Phibsborough, Dublin 7

Formerly known as the Arthur Conan Doyle, this Victorian public house was built using stones from the nearby Saint Peter's Church and comes complete with its own well in the cellar. It was frequented by the famous Irish writer Brendan Behan and was a personal favourite of the world-renowned hangman, Albert Pierrepoint. Doyles is in close proximity to Mountjoy prison so when he was in Dublin for 'work', Albert would pop in for a whiskey or two. The pub used to have Lanigans Funeral Home beside it for many years, which could account for the ghost who has taken residence and terrorized patrons on the second floor. It could also be one of Mr. Pierrepoint's 'work' subjects from Mountjoy, looking for the hangman!

John Mulligans, 8 Poolbeg Street, Dublin 2

Famous for featuring in one of the short stories of James Joyce, Counterparts, Mulligans has had more than its fair share of famous clientele. These days it is frequented by journalists and writers, who take solace in the subdued Victorian decor. Not just having to listen to the woes of dejected press members or massaging the egos of famous patrons, the bar staff have to contend with spirits and not of the top shelf variety! Flying brandy bottles, strange banging from the cellar and even the apparition of a man sitting on a beer barrel are just a few of the regular paranormal encounters at Mulligans.

Darkey Kelly's, 19 Fishamble Street, Christchurch, Dublin 2

Darkey Kelly was a convicted witch and Dublin's first known serial killer. Running a brothel on Fishamble Street, Darkey came to the attention of the authorities after accusing Simon Luttrell, Sheriff and member of the notorious Hellfire Club, of making her pregnant. Stories abound regarding the child being sacrificed on Montpelier Hill, however it was the discovery of at least five male corpses in her cellars that led to her arrest. Luttrell's input had the charges increased to witchcraft and she was executed. Darkey seems to remain, as patrons often feel watched, hear strange noises and objects move of their own volition.

Dublin's Haunted Fair City

As the song goes, Dublin's fair city is home to the ghost of Molly Malone who continues to wander the streets broad and narrow – she is not alone. Here are just a few of the most visited places in Dublin and the ghosts that dwell within.

Marsh's Library, St Patrick's Close, Dublin 8

The library founded by Archbishop Narcissus Marsh is over 300 years old. It is almost unique in that it remains in use in accordance with its original purpose and was frequented by Bram Stoker and Jonathan Swift. The walls are lined with over 2,5000 books and more than 300 rare manuscripts, placed in bookcases of dark solid oak, never changing.

Although English, Archbishop Marsh was given the title of Provost at Trinity College, Dublin and promoted the use and study of the Irish Language. To preserve Marsh's love of study and collection of books and manuscripts from around the world, he founded the library beside St Patrick's Cathedral.

Narcissus spent much of his remaining time within the confines of his book lined sanctuary while taking on the role of guardian for his niece. When she fell in love with a curate and eloped against his wishes, Marsh was heartbroken and on receiving a letter of explanation of her actions, placed it in a book, unable to read it at that time. The heartbroken Archbishop died soon after and is now seen wandering through the stacks, searching for the elusive book that contains the letter he never read.

St Michan's Church, Church Street, Dublin 7

This Church of Ireland place of worship has been on the same Viking site since 1095 A.D. Once again, a haunt for Bram Stoker, this architecturally stunning building is visited for very different reasons – the crypt.

The vaults beneath St Michan's have created a unique set of circumstances, which has left the corpses mummified. No caskets have been opened here. The strange environment means that while the coffins are rotting and falling away, the bodies within are perfectly preserved.

Well not quite perfectly – as there was a one size fits all policy for coffin making, various limbs have been hacked off and bent at odd angles to ensure the deceased would fit, leaving body parts jutting out from the confines of their final resting place.

There are four main caskets on view while the others are stacked in a macabre manner. One is simply referred to as the unknown woman, another as the nun. The thief is so named as his feet and right hand have been severed, although this may just have been to make him fit!

The Crusader is by far the most well visited corpse, his six and half foot frame astounding for a man from some few hundred years ago. His arm and finger protrude from his coffin and it is said that if you touch it you will have good fortune.

But be wary, you may well feel an ethereal touch of your own or hear whispers and disembodied voices as you visit the crypts of St Michan's.

Trinity College, College Green, Dublin 2

The flagship of Irish Academia, Trinity College was established at the end of the 16th century and covers nearly 50 acres of ground. Trinity has been a highly recognised centre of excellence for the study of medicine for centuries as well as having some extremely notable students in other disciplines, such as Bram Stoker (him again!) who studied here from 1864 – 1870. The Dublin University is also the guardian of major artefacts and manuscripts including the *Book of Kells*, so it of little surprise to find Trinity College has faculty members who have not let death stop them occupying the prestigious campus.

Narcissus Marsh of course prefers to spend time in his library, both alive and dead, however another Fellow of the College interfered too much in student life and paid for it with his life. Edward Ford was disliked by the students and one night, the 7th of March 1734, saw a group of rowdy gentlemen barge through the Front Gate, attacking a porter in the process. Unhappy at being admonished by Ford, they returned later to break the windows of his apartment in the Rubrics building.

Outraged, Edward fired his pistol into the crowd, slightly wounding a student. Angered further, the mob acquired their own weapons and shot Edward Ford dead as he screamed at them through his open window. The disgruntled Professor can be seen to this day, in full wig and gown, walking the paths until he simply dissipates as he approaches the Botany Bay area of the college.

Of course, as a medical teaching facility, new ground was looking to be broken and Trinity was not without tales of body snatching. In fact, when a new extension was being built, dismembered bodies and body parts dating back to the 18th Century were found as they dug out foundations which have been attributed to overzealous medical students. Perhaps they were inspired by the Head of the Medical School, Dr. Samuel Crossey, a man who was known for his brilliance as a medical teacher and trained many of the world's leading doctors and surgeons of the time.

Samuel Crossey however was also infamous for his nocturnal habits. At a time where cadavers were scarce, he was believed to have sourced his own. Not just from grave robbing either – in events that may have inspired Burke and Hare themselves, the bodies produced for dissection lectures were as likely to have been grabbed from the street as a grave. At least two students were also thought to have disappeared in mysterious circumstances. Death was not enough to stop Dr. Crossey continue his work, as his tall intimidating spectral figure can be seen crossing the quadrangles and paths of Trinity College, in one hand a surgeon's case and the other carries a rather conspicuous and chilling cloth sack.

Saint Patrick's Cathedral, Saint Patrick's Close, Dublin 8

The imposing Cathedral is built on what is believed to be the site of baptisms carried out by Saint Patrick in the fifth century when he visited Dublin. There are hundreds of bodies buried within the Cathedral and grounds, including those of Narcissus Marsh and Jonathan Swift.

Jonathan Swift's body was exhumed almost a century after his death and a post mortem took place to prove he had died from Meniere's disease and not insanity as first thought. His body was returned to its burial place and the Cathedral is also home to a mask of his skull and death masks. It is of little wonder therefore that the prolific author and clergyman is still seen within the building he called home.

The most famous ghost of Saint Patrick's is not human, but a Newfoundland dog. In 1861, a massive storm took place off the coast of what is now known as Dun Laoghaire, Dublin. A coal ship called *The Neptune* was in distress and going down, Captain John McNeill Boyd took the lifeboat *Ajax* out with five men to attempt to save the crew of *The Neptune*. All perished.

Each body was recovered immediately with the exception of the Captain of the *Ajax*. For weeks each day, his dog would join the search team until he was found. The distraught animal followed the funeral cortege dutifully to the place of interment in the grounds of Saint Patrick's Cathedral. Here the ghostly black canine remains, never to be separated from his master.

Dublin Castle, Palace Street, Dublin 2

Dublin Castle is not only a place of historical and political significance in Ireland, it is the location of source of the very naming of Dublin itself. Within the Castle, dating back to the Vikings lies a Black Pool, the Dubh Linn.

Since the Viking invasion until the Easter Rebellion, Dublin Castle has been the nerve centre for battles, military strategy and the persecution of a nation. It has as a result been the site of atrocities and the spirits of those who met horrific and untimely deaths at enemy hands remain. From the moment the Castle was reinforced with stone walls by King John of England at the start of the 13th century, the heads of would be conquering and invading forces were spiked onto it as a deterrent to potential enemies, the bodies left to rot beneath. The dungeons were witness to some of the most heinous cases of torture and murder of Catholics for no other reason than their faith. Clergymen were subject to every unspeakable act of cruelty including their feet being lowered into vats of boiling oil.

One woman, a widow in her late 70's who refused to renounce her faith, was left to starve to death in a cell by the Mayor of Dublin, her own son - her heartbroken spirit left to cry in despair for eternity in her prison.

In 1316 Roger de Fynglas was a career criminal was sentenced to hang; however, in a cruel twist his sentence was replaced with the more callous "to stay without food until dead." He remains within the dungeon, dwelling on his actions and fate.

When the Easter Rising took place in 1916, Commandant of the Dublin Brigade, James Connolly was seriously wounded. Captured, he was taken to Dublin Castle and kept for a week in a room now known as the James Connolly Room. Despite his wounds being mortal, James Connolly was dragged to Kilmainham Gaol where he was tied to a chair and executed by firing squad. His final days are imprinted firmly on the Castle and his presence is as much a part of Dublin Castle as the walls themselves.

Death, Haunting and the Blood Red Rose of Ballyseede Castle

Just off the main N69 Tralee/Killarney Road, three miles outside of Tralee stands the majestic Ballyseede Castle. Covering some 30 acres and approached from the road via a sweeping drive, the Castle is now a majestic four-star hotel and favourite wedding venue; however its current status is far removed from the dark and violent history for which it has notoriety. It is little wonder that it ranks so highly among in the world's most haunted hotels.

Built by the Fitzgerald family, the Castle was their garrison for what became known as the Geraldine Wars during the late 16th Century. Gerald Fitzgerald, 16th Earl of Desmond joined the Rebellion in defiance of the English and the Fitzgerald family openly refused to swear their allegiance to the Queen.

After years of fighting, Gerald was captured in Stacks Mountains, the range that dominates the Tralee skyline. Charged with treason to the crown, on 11th November 1583 he was taken to the Demesne at Ballyseede and beheaded by the local executioner, Daniel Kelly. As a warning to others not to disobey Queen Elizabeth, Gerald Fitzgerald's head was taken to London and was exhibited in a cage at London Bridge.

The Crown instructed the Governor of Kerry, Sir Edward Denny to lease what was then 3000 acres of estate at Ballyseede over to Thomas Blennerhassett of Cumberland, England in 1590. The unique annual rent was six pounds and a single red rose to be picked from the Castle gardens on Midsummer's Day. Although remaining in the Blennerhassett family, the once proud castle fell into disrepair until the early 18th century when William, son of the former leassee, took it upon himself to build the current imposing structure.

Upon William's death, the entire estate was bequeathed to his son Arthur, who at the very young age of 21 was appointed High Sheriff of Kerry, leading to a successful political career. It was during this time that the Castle was expanded, and the grounds landscaped further. Arthur married the daughter of the Knight of Glin from the neighbouring county of Limerick and they had a daughter called Hilda who went on to become a nurse. During the First World War she was awarded the 1914 Mons Star, an honour usually given to male officers, however Hilda was one of a handful of nurses to receive the medal for her work in France and Belgium.

Hilda however, had not seen the last of the bloodshed and horror of war. In 1923, just two years after the Irish War of Independence and just one year after the death of Michael Collins, a quartermaster of the IRA issued an order for the death of Free State Army Lieutenant Paddy O'Connor.

On the 6th of March, the unsuspecting Officer was decoyed to Knocknagoshel and a mine trap, where he and five of his unit were killed outright. Outraged, the Free State took immediate retaliatory steps. IRA prisoners were being held at Ballymullen Barracks in Tralee, so shortly before dawn the following day, nine were removed and taken to Ballyseede Crossroads, close to the Castle.

The road itself had been barricaded with rocks, tree trunks and explosives. The prisoners were bound, then forced to stand against the blockade, at which point the command to detonate was given. Not satisfied that all the prisoners were all dead, a further orde was given, and the mutilated men were subjected to machine gun fire in the shadows of Ballyseede Castle gates.

A cross stands at the gates in their memory and a bronze memorial known as the Ballyseede Monument stands further along the road in honour of Irish Republicanism. Hilda herself died in 1965 and was buried next to her family members in nearby Ballyseede Graveyard. In keeping with her persona, there is a simple cross marking her grave. Hilda was the last of the Blennerhassett bloodline and the Estate was put up for auction. The single red rose that had kept Ballyseede Castle in the Blennerhassett family for almost four hundred years was no more.

The Castle was converted into a hotel; however one particular member of the Blennerhassett family was checked in as a permanent ghost. Hilda has regularly been seen and indeed conversed with in the hotel, particularly in the Crosby room, which had been hers. Despite legend having Hilda appear on the 24th of March each year, she has been seen much more frequently. Interestingly since Hilda's passing, roses have never been present in the hotel, however on the top floor, the strong scent of roses can be noticed. Hilda herself can be seen at her window looking out across the grounds and beneath her window the letters RIP eerily appears and then vanishes.

The staff at Ballyseede have had many of their own experiences. However, one staff member named Esther has had more than her fair share. Esther had been stock taking and had sole access to the premises. As she approached the Castle along the drive, she could clearly see a shadow at Hilda's window and it appeared that the television and lights were on. After unlocking the door and dashing up the stairs, Esther rushed into the Crosby room to discover everything was turned off. Almost as if to let Esther know it wasn't her imagination, this occurrence repeated itself the following day.

On another occasion two ladies who were staying in the Crosby room were dining in the Stoneroom, being served by a young girl called Paige. The ladies had told her that Hilda had been talking to them and so Paige asked Esther if she could go to the room and see for herself.

A while later Paige returned, white as a sheet and told Esther that Hilda had spoken with her. The former nurse had told Paige she would be gone from the hotel within the year and overseas. Less than twelve months later Paige was working in England.

Of course, Hilda isn't the only spirit to wander the halls of this stately home. Former landlords keep a careful watch on the upkeep of Ballyseede and undoubtedly those who were executed or died in battle remain in the grounds, or in nearby Ballyseede woods where the original house once stood.

I recently had the opportunity to stay in this magnificent building and whilst I did not encounter Hilda, I witnessed enough to know that the living are not the only guests at Ballyseede Castle, however only the living check out.

Charles Fort, Kinsale and the Lady in White

In the south west of Ireland, the medieval fishing port of Kinsale stands on the mouth of the River Bandon in County Cork. With a rich and varied history, this quaint tourist village with its labyrinth of narrow streets is set firmly between the hills and shoreline, little having changed in centuries.

Built in the late 17th century, Charles Fort in the Summer Cove part of Kinsale was designed as a star fortification by the Surveyor General of Ireland to maximise defence from cannon attack from the water or land. This stronghold was witness to many historical events and battles from the Williamite War of 1689/91 to the War of Independence, all taking place in its shadow.

Of particular note is that it played host to Admiral Penn, the Governor of Kinsale, placed there by force after turning traitor to the Crown, taking orders from Cromwell and failing in his task to take the West Indies cleanly for the Commonwealth. The Admiral had a son called William who became the Clerk to the Admiralty Court of Kinsale during his time in Ireland, after which he journeyed to America and became the founder of Pennsylvania.

Kinsale has many stories and I am about to tell you one of its most famous - that of the Lady in White. The Commander of Charles Fort at the time in question was believed to be named Warrender. He had a daughter who lead a life of privilege in the town of Kinsale and remained mostly within the garrison itself. Under English rule, the barracks had a turnover of soldiers and a young touring Officer fell in love with the Commander's daughter and she with him. After a whirlwind romance the two were betrothed and married.

After a wedding day of festivities, later that night, duties returned to normal as Charles Fort was still of course an operational garrison. The newlyweds took an evening walk along the parapets and the young bride was soon distracted by a single white flower growing below.

An eager young sentry stated he would climb down the ramparts and fetch the flower as a wedding gift if her Officer husband would mind his post. The groom took up the post with the sentry's musket and waited…and waited…

With no sign of the sentry, quite possibly an absconder, the newly married Officer sent his dear wife to their chambers while he stood guard. Tired after a day of drinking and excitement he gradually dozed off, leaning on the musket.

Later that night the Commander took to his rounds and found the sleeping soldier. As the offence demanded immediate resolution and penalty, the Commander raised his gun and fired, only realising the moment he released the trigger that he was shooting his own son- in- law in the heart.

Distraught over his actions and unable to face the grief and judgement of his daughter, in a split-second decision the Commander threw himself from the battlements.

The young wife awoke from a short sleep and went in search of her husband, only to find his bloody corpse. In despair she looked out over the ramparts and saw the broken body of her father below. This was all too much for the new bride to take in and so she leapt broken hearted to her death.

From that day her lonely spirit, dressed in her wedding gown wanders the parapets of the Fort, desperate and forlorn and can be seen as the evening turns to night. Her eerie presence casts fear and sorrow into those who see her, and until it was abandoned, leaving even the battle-hardened soldiers of the Fort to carry out their duties in terror, locking all the doors to keep her from entering. A futile gesture, as this grief-stricken widow who lost the two men she loved has nowhere else to go.

Gentry, Gallows and Ghosts at Ardoginna House

This Castle styled property dating back to the early 17th century goes by many names including Ardo House, McKenna's Castle and the formal Ardoginna House. One title is constant, however, and that is as one of the creepiest ruins in Ireland.

Ardoginna House is situated in the fishing village of Ardmore in County Waterford. The first documented owner of this imposing property was James Fitzgerald. However, there have been many changes of hands throughout the centuries, each having its own share of trouble. There are those who believe firmly that Ardoginna House is rooted in evil and ill fortune.

In 1619, the Fitzgerald family granted a lease to Pierce Power, who added the name of Richard Costen as his heir to the deed. One night the young man saw fit to steal a precious metal object from his guardians and took flight from his home. Richard was chased mercilessly by members of the household staff across the cliff tops of the coastal village of Ardmore. At one point, his horse reared up and threw the heir from the saddle whereby he was caught in his steed's reins and hanged. An alternative tale claims Richard Costen was actually caught and hanged by his pursuers, however either way the area is now known as 'Croch an Oidhre' or 'The Heir's Gallows.' Local tales say he can still be seen trying to ride his horse to safety.

Prior to the turn of the 18th century, the grand estate became the primary residence of Sir Francis Prendergast, who was known for his callous and indeed somewhat psychotic personality. Those in his employ worked and lived in the property in a constant state of terror, as he had hanged a servant with whom he was displeased and buried the unfortunate soul under the dining room. Their skeletal remains were exhumed some decades later, along with the bones of a small child found underneath the stairs. The spectre of the evil landlord of Ardoginna House can be found wandering the estate after dark.

The Coghlan family took ownership and in 1795, the eldest daughter married into English nobility of the highest order. This was not enough to change the turning tide of the family's finances however and the resourceful widow and head of Ardoginna House made use of the quiet coastline by turning to smuggling to maintain her lifestyle and support two of her children who had been born with deformities.

The title of McKenna's Castle came about when Joseph Neale McKenna became the landlord of the estate in 1865. With macabre and opulent taste, the owner had built an enormous mausoleum on the land that could be viewed from the house while he and his wife were still living. The vault included carvings and a large statue of an angel shadowing over the whole burial ground. After they had both passed away at the start of the 20th century, Joseph McKenna's extravagance became his undoing. Looking for hidden treasures and taking marble and stone, graverobbers completely defiled the tomb, however the angel remains in the undergrowth, keeping a stony watch on the ruins of its master's castle.

Grief, Ghosts and Gothic Revival At Duckett's Grove

Although only ruins now, the outline of the towers and turrets of Duckett's Grove stand resplendent against the horizon and surrounding countryside of the estate to which they have belonged for nearly two centuries. Duckett's Grove was originally a modest two-story house built in the style of its day in the mid-18th century by a descendent of the Duckett family, who arrived to the townland of Kneestown in County Carlow some 100 years previously.

As the family grew in wealth and social standing in both Carlow and Dublin city, it became clear that the somewhat ordinary family home was insufficient to meet the Duckett needs. The owner, William Duckett married an heiress by the name of Harriet to further his aspirations of grandeur.

In 1830 therefore, the services of Thomas A. Cobden, renowned architect were secured, and work began on making Duckett Grove a Gothic revival masterpiece of epic proportion, with regal arches, neo-gothic oriel windows and grotesques added to the majestic towers and imposing structure.

Now believing his home was suitable for his social needs, William Duckett began to throw lavish parties inviting the socialites of Dublin to mingle with local gentry and the Duckett family. William was somewhat of a philanderer and married his second wife, Maria Thompson in 1895 when he was 73 years old, bringing her and her daughter Olive to reside at Duckett's Grove. William passed away in 1908 and was buried in the family plot at nearby Knocknacree. Maria continued to live in solitude at the mock Gothic Castle as she and her daughter had become estranged. Finally, Maria abandoned the property in 1916 to live in Dublin.

In a twist, when Maria died she was so furious with Olive, that in her will she left nothing but what was known as the 'Angry Shilling' to her absentee offspring. Not wishing to be done out of her inheritance, Olive went to court and in a week and a half long hearing, it was revealed that mother and daughter had a tempestuous and physically violent relationship, much to the shock of the Dublin city social scene. Maria was given a cash settlement and the Ducketts of Duckett's Grove were no more.

Originally purchased by a farmer's collective, bickering and greed over shares led to default on payment and the Land Commission stepped in and took over. During this time in the early 1920's the IRA made use of Duckett's Grove for training purposes and it was the base of its flying column, a mobile armed unit of soldiers. Despite the nature of its use post-Duckett, the great house was well maintained until it was brought to a smoking shell by way of a catastrophic fire on 20 April 1933 – the cause of which was never discovered.

Although nothing but a husk, it would seem that the events within Duckett's Grove have left their mark, with several agitated spirits being witnessed over the decades, making the building ruins a hotspot for numerous paranormal investigations, including America's *Destination Truth* in 2011.

The most notorious entity identified is the Duckett's Grove Banshee. Banshees have forever been known as portents of death, with most connected to families and more than a few of these wailing spirits seeking death for revenge and torment. In this instance, the Banshee is the result of a *Piseóg*, a curse placed on the house and family to bring about death, despair and financial ruin. This particular curse was cast by the angry grieving mother of a young girl who had been having an affair with William Duckett and was riding on the estate when she fell from her horse.

The bringer of death can be heard shrieking on the wind through the ruins of Duckett's Grove from the towers for two days and nights, with stories of those that heard her suffering fatality and family tragedy. Noted accounts include a woman who dropped dead in the grounds and a worker in the gardens who heard the feared cry and whose mother died the follow morning. Servants have distinctly been heard working in what was formerly the kitchens, and a phantom horse and carriage has rolled up to the former entrance.

Disembodied voices, bangs, floating balls of light and spectral shadows are just a few more of the paranormal phenomena to occur in the Carlow castle. Apparitions of various figures, believed to be members of the Duckett family have been seen, including what is believed to be the ghost of William Duckett himself, riding a horse on his estate.

The Ducketts' had extremely strong ties to the Protestant Church and a vocalised hatred of Catholicism, so some investigators have provoked heightened paranormal responses from the entities of Duckett's Grove, by bringing Catholic relics such as rosary beads to investigations.

Now Duckett's Grove is open to the public, with visitors touring the extensive gardens and woodlands. For those who look at the Gothic skeleton that remains, it is a statuesque reminder of the opulent and lavish lifestyle that used to be lived within. For those who are braver, the ruins provide a hive of paranormal occurrences to be witnessed from the brightest and busiest of tourist days to the dead of night.

With a family history of materialism, violence and infidelity, and with the Duckett family motto of 'Let us be judged by our acts', it is little wonder therefore that this noble family and those whose lives they touched remain the eternally restless residents of Duckett's Grove.

The Phantom Corpse of Sopwell Hall

The property was formerly known as Kinelagh Castle, an ancestral home of a local clan and was seized by Cromwellian forces. In the mid-17th century, Cromwell handed the land to General Thomas Sadleir. This was passed down and in the mid-18th century Sopwell Hall was built as a reminder of the grand Sopwell house in Hertfordshire, England by Colonel Francis Sadleir.

When Francis was dying he informed his son he wanted no pomp or circumstance, however his son disagreed, and they fought until he died. While drinking over his father's corpse, in a drunken rage he and a friend unceremoniously grabbed the coffin from where it lay and dragged it towards the top of the stairs and proceeded downward. In their inebriated state they slipped and the coffin with Colonel Sadleir inside crashed down the stairs. Anyone who has ventured in has heard a soul-wrenching scream followed by the sound of a dead weight being dragged down the staircase. A disrespected spirit refusing to rest.

Annagh Castle and the Guarded Treasure

Lough Derg is the largest lake within the Shannon region and means 'Lake of the Red Eye'. On the banks of Lough Derg stand the ruins of Annagh Castle, built in the 16th century and once home to the English politician, Sir Phillip Perceval, however his is not the spirit that wanders the castle remains.

Former owner, Edmund Roe O'Kennedy was brutally murdered by enemy forces before he could tell a soul where he had hidden his treasure. He can be seen wandering the ruins, his face a grotesque death mask, his neck gaping open, wound bloodied and congealed. In 1975, an archaeology student was disturbed from digging by the sound of a gasping moan and came face to face with the hideous shade of Edmund Roe O'Kennedy. Even after all these years Edmund seems to be determined that no one will find his treasure and death will not stop him.

The Druid's Curse of Moorehall

Overlooking Lough Carra in County Mayo, stands the burned-out family manor of one of the most influential families in Ireland. A shell that has touched on the worst parts of Irish history and was said to have been built on an ancient curse.

George Henry Moore was a prominent Irish Politician in the 18th century and both he and his descendants rose to distinction in military, political and cultural fields. Moore himself emigrated to Spain following the implementation of the penal laws and rose to prominence gaining a place in the Spanish Court. He set up a business trading in brandy and fine wines, which afforded him the luxury of having enough money to build his own mansion upon returning to Ireland.

With many sites to choose from, George Moore settled on Muckloon Hill overlooking Lough Carra. Locals vehemently warned against such a location as the land was deemed to be cursed.

In around 400 A.D the King of Connacht, Brian Orbsen was slain by his enemies. The King's Druid, Drithliu, however made good his escape. He sought sanctuary on Muckloon Hill but failed to outrun his pursuers who caught up with him and Drithliu bled out on the shores of the Lough. The stubborn landowner went ahead regardless and Moorehall was built by Waterford Cathedral architect John Roberts, with Moore taking up residency in 1795. Shortly afterwards George Henry Moore suffered a stroke and was left blind. And so, the curse of Moorehall had begun.

George's son John trained as a lawyer and was made President of Connacht which was a Republic at the time of his commission in 1798. Unfortunately, his position was a short-lived affair following the appointment of Command-In-Chief of Ireland, the 1st Marquess Cornwallis in direct response to the Irish Rebellion. John was arrested by the Lord Lieutenant and was given the death penalty. George Moore used some of his fortune to secure the best lawyers he could find and had his son's sentence commuted to a deportation order. While on remand awaiting the transport ship John succumbed to the injuries he sustained in custody. Just a few months later George Moore was also dead. The curse had struck again.

The next owner of Moorehall was also named George Henry Moore. His money was made in horseracing yet not without tragedy. In 1845 his brother Augustus was jockeying a horse by the name of Mickey Free in the English Grand National. He fell from his horse during the race and died. George himself won the Gold Cup the following year and used the money to buy grain and cattle for his famine struck tenants. It was documented that not one of the people on Moore land became victims of the Famine.

George Augustus Moore was to be the last resident owner of Moorehall and the great grandson of the man who had built the very same. Born in 1852, he went on to study the arts and become a prolific writer as well as a founder of the Abbey Theatre. George's social circle included Oscar Wilde, folklorist Lady Gregory and occultist and esteemed writer W. B Yeats, all regular visitors to his grand ancestral home.

While George was residing in England at the height of the Irish Civil War, the anti-treaty IRA took umbrage at his cousin Maurice's political stance and after commandeering Moorehall, set the mansion with explosives and burned it out. Was this the final part of the curse? Apparently not.

The facade remains, exposed to the elements. Creeping tentacles of ivy crawl through the dark soulless voids where the windows once reflected the beauty of the sky and the Lough. If you pass through the undergrowth and the age weary tunnel at the rear of the once majestic building, you can see the lowest level of Moorehall, left much as it was in 1923, whatever remains within peering up into the 21st century sky.

Visitors to the cursed site describe ominous sensations and the overwhelming feeling that they are being watched by some unseen presence. There have been reports of hearing children's laughter and seeing shadows darting through the remaining structure. The woods themselves that encompass the fallen noble home are said to have an oppressive and foreboding silence within them.

Historic tragedy has befallen the residents of Moorehall over generations, which has directly led to accounts of paranormal activity within the ruins and the tale of a serpent like creature known as a *péist* dwelling in the waters of Lough Carra. It should also not be forgotten that the Moore family are interred close by in their ancestral vault. Included is John Moore whose body was not located until the mid-20th century where he was brought home and laid with his kin following a full military send off.

Could the murder of an ancient Druid on Muckloon Hill have created a curse so strong that is has spiralled down through the centuries? Is part of that curse that the Moores remain in residence for eternity? No one will ever know for sure. No one but a Druid named Drithliu.

Ghost Children of Ireland

For centuries, the spooky Irish landscape has been home to tales of ghostly infants and adolescents, causing more fear and discomfort than all of the adult hauntings combined.

From the disembodied cry of a young boy calling out for his Daddy in Cork Gaol, to the image of a demented young girl, staggering around, blood dripping from her hands at Athcarne Castle in County Meath, nothing is quite as hair-raising and unnerving as a spectral child.

Ballyvourney De Salle College, Cork

De Salle College was an all-boys boarding school that closed to students in 1989. The subject of paranormal investigation, the now abandoned buildings are said to be haunted by several apparitions including a young boy and four teachers. In the deserted corridors, the eerie sounds of children laughing, and a school bell ringing can be heard, so school is still very much in session at De Salle College.

Old Castle Ruins, Castlelyons, Cork

Built in the 17th century and also known as Barrymore Castle, the imposing structure remained home to generations of the Barrymore family until it was destroyed by fire in 1771 and never restored.

The fire was not enough, however, to keep away the tragic figure of a phantom youth known as the Begging Boy. The wretched child wanders the ruins, begging for his life, cruelly repeating his last moments before he was murdered by one of the Castle residents for disobedience.

Charleville Forest Castle, Offaly

Charleville Forest Castle was built in the early 19th century, designed by the architect responsible for the famous G.P.O. in Dublin.

The daughter of the 3rd Earl of Charleville, Harriet died aged eight in 1861 after sliding down the main balustrade and losing her grip, crashing to the stone floor. Her ghost can still be seen, and she is feltushing past startled visitors on the stairs. At night the screams, laughter and singing of a young girl are heard along with the sounds of children at play echoing in the nursery.

Renvyle House Hotel, Connemara, Galway

Nestled away in rural Galway, Renvyle House was built in 1883 and became a haven for poets, artisans and politicians after it was purchased by Oliver St. John Gogarty. W.B Yeats became a regular visitor and picked up on the fact that the property was a hive of paranormal activity.

Curious to find out more, Yeats, Gogarty and friends began to try and connect with the spirits and during one séance the figure of a teenage boy appeared out of the mist. Believed to be a member of the Blake family who constructed the grand house, the vision lurched around, wide eyed and clutching his hands to his throat.

College Lane, Clane, Kildare

On the road just outside Clongowes Wood College, several motorists have been forced to grind to a screeching halt, heart in mouth. Each one saw a child appear without warning on the road in front of them and had to take evasive action.

Once the shock had subsided they would jump from their vehicles and search for the child, only to find the youngster had completely vanished.

Rhetoric House, Maynooth College, Kildare

Founded in the late 18th century and originally a Seminary for the instruction of priests, Maynooth College began accepting lay people for study in 1968. Still educating students for the priesthood, despite the Catholic influence, evil remained very much within its walls.

Stories of demonic activity and other paranormal occurrences were rife over the centuries and two students committed suicide out of fear, claiming to have been witness to a threatening malevolent entity - both residents of Rhetoric House. Both suicides involved slashing with a razor blade with the last one throwing himself from his window. The young lad survived long enough to say he had seen the face of a demon reflected in the mirror and a powerful, evil force engulfed him, controlling his mind and forcing him to harm himself.

Following the revelations of the unfortunate student, a priest took it upon himself to enter Rhetoric House and face the darkness of Room Two. After spending the night and not emerging, concerned faculty found him trembling in the corner of the room, incoherent and terrified, his hair turned white overnight.

Both students were buried in unconsecrated ground within the Campus, but whether their tormented spirits have ever left, Room Two is very much in question.

Ireland's Scariest Poltergeists

Although stories of poltergeists have been associated with properties going back centuries in Ireland, proper accounts and media interest have been limited largely due to the fear of being accused of demon possession and occultism in this predominantly Catholic country.

It is surprising therefore, to find that the worst of Ireland's poltergeist reports are all with in recent memory, some very recent indeed. More astonishing is that most of them are private residences, where the distress and trepidation of living with a paranormal entity far outweighed the fear of public ridicule and accusations, leading members of the terrorized families to publicise their accounts.

Court Street, Enniscorthy, County Wexford

In July 1910, the most a lodger would have to worry about was having enough shillings to make rent. However, this was not the case for a man called Randell who shared board with two other lodgers and the family of the house.

Activity began with the pulling of bedclothes, but soon escalated into the dragging of beds across the room, chairs rocking and sliding of their own accord, disembodied footsteps and pounding sounds throughout the lodgings.

Such was the fear in the household that local sceptics were called in to disprove the phenomena as hysteria, but they were unsuccessful.

Finally, after just three weeks that culminated in the boarders being tossed from their beds onto the floor, Randell left the premises, terrified and almost a stone lighter from his ordeal. It was at this point that the activity ceased.

18 Hollywood Estate, Hollyhill, Cork

In 2010, a young family contacted the local media for help as they were being terrorized in their home by an unseen entity. What began as minor annoyances such as missing items and strange sounds, soon took a nasty turn for Laura Burke, her fiancé Richie and son Kyle.

Holy pictures were forcefully removed from the walls, time and time again. Furniture would shake and crash and clothes would be launched from wardrobes and drawers. Screams would be heard in the dead of night and the climax was young Kyle being levitated and thrown from his bed. Terrified, the young family resorted to living with relatives as the council refused to rehouse them.

With the assistance of a local radio station, Shaman Paul O'Halloran was called in and he detected hundreds of spirits trapped in the house, including children and famine victims. Whatever transpired after that remains inconclusive, but the family never returned and the house remains boarded up and empty - of the living at least.

Corrib Park, Galway

When the Fahy family welcomed a granddaughter into their home, they had no idea of the horror they were about to unleash. Baby Sarah Louise was brought to the house in 1996 and that was the catalyst for a tirade of paranormal activity.

At first, there was a strong smell of urine that would occur room by room. Ornaments would shatter and the bloodcurdling screams of a young child were heard in the night.

The Fahys knew when they were being visited by this restless spirit as the temperature of their home would plummet to freezing, after which time the knocking and smashing of objects would begin.

On speaking with locals, they discovered the house was built on old farmland and it is believed a man of the cloth fathered a child and murdered the same on that very spot to cover up his indiscretion. Fearing for the safety of their grandchild, a spiritualist was called in to perform a healing and cleansing ceremony during which time the spirit of an infant was seen rising into the light and fading from view.

Olympia Theatre, 72 Dame Street, Dublin, D2

Originally known as The Star of Erin, Dublin's Olympia Theatre was opened in 1878. Artists from Laurel and Hardy to Noel Coward and Alec Guinness have all performed in the Victorian building but there are some acts that prefer to be heard and not seen.

Poltergeist activity has been rife throughout the decades with stories of doors and windows rattling violently, ghostly footsteps echoing throughout and the violent destruction of a dressing room by an unseen entity.

First-hand accounts of her own terrifying encounters have been told by long time employee Maureen Grant. Her first experience of the poltergeist was when she was changing for a shift. Stood in just her underwear about to wash, the door to the bathroom shot open. Maureen closed it and as she turned to continue, the door rattled and banged and her uniform flew off the door hook.

A traumatized Maureen fled, grabbing her coat for decency and tore into the café. The fear increased as it dawned on her that the employee she suspected of playing a prank was in fact seated having a meal. This was the beginning of a host of occurrences that saw lights switching on without being connected and the sound of a baby crying. A medium was brought in, however this just seemed to amplify the activity.

Focus moved to the bar now known as Maureen's Bar, with glasses smashing and money jumping around in the cash registers, terrorising staff. It would appear the Olympia Theatre Poltergeist is settled in for a long residency.

Residential House, Kilmallock, County Limerick

A young man by the name of Callum recounted the terror that visited his family circa 2006. Immediately after his sister sustained a minor head trauma, she began to be tormented with blankets being taken and being ousted by an unseen force from her bed.

She became sickly and was ordered bed rest, during which time the poltergeist activity became stronger but completely focused on the terrified youngster. Banging sounds echoed continually round the bedroom, to the point where neighbours complained. After the sibling recovered, activity settled, however relief was to be short lived. The bed started to elevate and drop, pictures would catapult from the walls and furniture would move around.

Concerned for the safety of their children, the parents sent them to live with family. However the activity followed so they returned home. When the activity grew more violent and Callum's sister was getting dragged around and targeted by flying objects, priests were called in to cleanse the house and the girl, leading to the subsiding of poltergeist activity until it ceased altogether a few months later.

His claims have not been substantiated by any other source in part due to the privacy of the family and the reluctance of the Catholic Church to admit to such events. Whether a fanciful teen or genuine activity, we will never know for sure, however the town of Kilmallock is built on centuries of violence and bloodshed. With that much ferocious energy echoing around the medieval stone walled parish, it is quite within the realms of possibility that some was unleashed and attached itself to an innocent young girl as she banged her head on the ground.

ACKNOWLEGEMENTS

Well there you have it, some of my Dark Emerald Tales. There are more that simply would not fit and more still to be written, so look out for Volume 2!

The journey to this finished book has been long, fun and inspirational. There are so many people I must thank for getting me here. My Dad Danny (RIP), whose artistic gene I thankfully inherited! My mum Elizabeth, for getting me started on this road in childhood, with her own stories and love of the written word. As a child my best friend was always the next book. My stepdad James (RIP), whose love of storytelling was something special and who always encouraged me and wanted me to do what makes me happy.

Thank you, David Saunderson, Spooky Isles for having faith in me, being so supportive and a fantastic mentor and awesome friend. For Mandy, I'm a writer who does not have the words to say what your friendship and guidance has meant to me. You are also a very patient publisher!

Thank you to those in my life who have nudged me from day one to reach for the stars and follow my heart, offering help along the way. Thank you to my amazing family and friends who have always shown interest in my work, reading, sharing and encouraging all the time.

I want to thank my best friend for helping me find focus, strength and determination in difficult times and helping me find the best of me while keeping me calm – not an easy feat. Procrastination and letting the wind get taken from my sails are negatives that happen all too easily for me, so having that positive, calm energy holding my hand has been a blessing.

Also thank you for your annoying attention to detail that has helped me become a better writer!

For my daughter Siobhan, believe in magic always, it keeps the darkness out and hope, passion and inspiration alive.

In memory of my wonderful son Daniel. I never had the opportunity to tell you these tales and that is something I will always be sad about, but I know you are with me as I continue on my path of discovery and adventure.

http://www.mysteriousbritain.co.uk
http://www.historyireland.com
http://archive.archaeology.org
http://www.bbc.co.uk/history/scottishhistory/darkages
http://www.yourirish.com
https://myarmoury.com/

Malachi martin books
National Library Ireland
Lady Gregory

(Excerpt from 'The Stolen Child' by W.B Yeats)

True Irish Ghost Stories

Many thanks to http://www.wicklowshistoricgaol.com

The Banshee

About the Author

Ann Massey O'Regan is an Irish folklore expert and Irish 'monster' scholar. She is Ireland Editor for Spooky Isles, a published Irish folk horror writer, Blogger at Dark Emerald Tales and contributed to numerous other international publications. She also sought out for research and analysis on the paranormal and folklore.

In addition, Ann is the Irish monster and folklore expert for WAYWARD comic, and has written for other international off beat projects including 'Outside In Takes a Stab', a quirky look at Buffy the Vampire Slayer.

In her spare time, Ann is a Paranormal Investigator with Irish Paranormal Investigations. As a team they investigate Ireland's most famous supernatural locations and many more hidden haunted gems off the beaten track.

Ann has a lifelong passion for writing and an obsession with the darker side of Ireland's history and heritage so the two were bound to intertwine some day!

Lightning Source UK Ltd.
Milton Keynes UK
UKHW012016081220
374848UK00005B/1430